TOP 10
MALTA & GOZO

MARY-ANN GALLAGHER

DK

EYEWITNESS TRAVEL

Left **Fish market, Marsaxlokk** Centre **Mnajdra Temple** Right **Historical re-enactment, Valletta**

LONDON, NEW YORK,
MELBOURNE, MUNICH AND DELHI
www.dk.com

Produced by Coppermill Books
55 Salop Road London E17 7HS
Printed and bound in China
First American Edition, 2007
15 16 17 18 10 9 8 7 6 5 4 3 2 1
Published in the United States by
DK Publishing, 345 Hudson Street,
New York, New York 10014

Reprinted with revisions 2009, 2011, 2013, 2015

Copyright © 2007, 2015
Dorling Kindersley Limited, London

A Penguin Random House Company

Published in the UK by Dorling Kindersley Limited

A catalog record for this book is available from
the Library of Congress.

ISSN 1479-344X
ISBN: 978-1-4654-2921-6

Within each Top 10 list in this book, no hierarchy
of quality or popularity is implied. All 10 are, in the
editor's opinion, of roughly equal merit.

Floors are referred to throughout in accordance
with British usage; ie the "first floor" is the floor
above ground level.

Town names used in the guide follow official
government use. These names may vary slightly
from local signs used in Malta, but are as up-to-
date as possible at the time of going to press.

MIX
Paper from
responsible sources
FSC
www.fsc.org   FSC™ C018179

Contents

Malta & Gozo's Top 10

Left **Golden Bay** Centre **Gobelin Tapestries, Grand Master's Palace** Right **Marina, Il-Birgu**

Left **Blue Lagoon, Comino** Right **Palazzo Parisio, In-Naxxar**

MALTA'S & GOZO'S TOP 10

TOP 10 Malta and Gozo Highlights

The tiny Maltese archipelago, floating on the cusp of Europe and Africa, has been coveted and invaded throughout its history. The Knights of St John (later of Malta) bequeathed palaces, fortresses and the glorious golden capital Valletta, while the British left red telephone boxes, iced buns and a predilection for tea. It was the islands' earliest settlers who left the most spectacular legacy: the extraordinary megalithic temples, unparalleled elsewhere in the world. Malta, the largest island, has the most cosmopolitan resorts and the edge in cultural treasures, while sleepy Gozo and tiny Comino offer unspoilt countryside and a gentler pace.

1 Grand Master's Palace, Valletta

This is a fittingly splendid home for the supreme head of the Knights. The opulent apartments are filled with treasures ranging from paintings and armour to elaborate friezes *(see pp8–9)*.

2 St John's Co-Cathedral, Valletta

This, one of the world's finest Baroque churches, still belongs to the Knights of Malta. The Oratory contains Caravaggio's masterpiece, *The Beheading of John the Baptist (see pp10–13)*.

3 Ħaġar Qim and Mnajdra

These hauntingly beautiful temples made of creamy limestone are set on a wild and rugged cliff-top overlooking the sea. Ħaġar Qim is fascinatingly complex, while Mnajdra's South Temple is the best preserved of all Malta's ancient sites *(see pp14–15)*.

4 L-Imdina and Ir-Rabat

L-Imdina, Malta's ancient capital, is a magical little city girdled by sturdy walls and full of medieval palaces and fine churches. Next-door Ir-Rabat boasts some of the most important Christian sites in Malta *(see pp16–17)*.

5 Palazzo Parisio, In-Naxxar

This splendid private palace was utterly transformed by the 2nd Marquis of Scicluna in the early years of the 20th century. Its opulent salons and glorious gardens were embellished by the finest craftsman from Malta and Italy *(see pp18–19)*.

Preceding pages **Armour of the Knights of St John, in the Armoury of the Grand Master's Palace, Valletta**

7 Hal Saflieni Hypogeum, Paola

More than 55 centuries ago, men hewed this extraordinary necropolis out of solid rock. The chambers are spread over three levels and are magnificently carved and decorated *(see pp22–3)*.

6 Marsaxlokk

In this enchanting little fishing village, traditional, brightly painted *luzzus* bob in the blue bay. Maltese families pour in on Sundays to visit the famous fish market on the quays, and then to linger in one of the excellent seafront restaurants *(see pp20–21)*.

8 The Citadel, Ir-Rabat/Victoria

The tiny walled Citadel sits high on a lofty promontory right in the centre of Gozo; from this vantage point, views unfold across the entire island and beyond to Malta. Within its walls is a clutch of fascinating museums *(see pp24–5)*.

Malta

9 Dwejra, Gozo

Gozo's wild, dramatic western coastline is spectacularly beautiful around Dwejra, where the huge Azure Window frames stunning views of the receding cliffs. It's perfect hiking territory, and the diving is among the best in the Med *(see pp26–7)*.

10 Comino

The smallest inhabited island in the Maltese archipelago, tiny Comino is an unspoilt wilderness where the air is still spicily scented with the cumin that gives it its name. You can swim in the Blue Lagoon or hike to spectacular cliffs *(see pp28–9)*.

Note that Malta and Gozo both have towns named Ir-Rabat.

🔟 Grand Master's Palace, Valletta

This handsome palace was built between 1573 and 1578 by the celebrated Maltese architect Gerolamo Cassar (1520–86), who was also responsible for the Co-Cathedral of St John. Today it is the President's office and seat of the Maltese Parliament, but for more than two hundred years it was the residence of the Grand Master, supreme head of the Order of the Knights of St John. Here, the Grand Master would greet foreign envoys and important guests, and the State Apartments are suitably crammed with reminders of the Order's fabulous wealth and influence. The palace's armoury contains a spectacular array of weaponry and armour spanning two centuries.

Supreme Council Hall

🕐 The Palace may be closed if Parliament is in session; check with the tourist office in advance.

🍴 There are numerous cafés in the vicinity. Drop into the elegant wine bar Ambrosia *(see p67)* for a delicious light meal.

- Triq Ir-Repubblika
- Map J2
- 2124 9349
- Palace: Open 10am–4pm Fri–Wed. Adm palace and armoury €10 (concessions €7, children under 11s €5)
- Armoury: Open 9am–5pm daily. Adm when palace state rooms closed €6 (concessions €4.50, children under 11s €3)
- Audio-guide free with admission ticket
- www.heritagemalta.org (armoury only)

Top 10 Features

1. Neptune's Courtyard
2. Corridors of the Knights
3. Tapestry Chamber
4. Gobelin Tapestries
5. Supreme Council Hall
6. Great Siege Frieze
7. Ambassador's Room
8. State Dining Hall
9. Armoury
10. Parade Armour

1 Neptune's Courtyard

The impressive statue that gives its name to the main courtyard *(below)* is attributed to the Flemish-born sculptor Giambologna (1529–1608). It is said that Admiral Andrea Doria, a friend of Grand Master de la Vallette, volunteered to pose naked for the statue.

2 Corridors of the Knights

On the first floor (the *piano nobile*) of the palace, lavishly decorated marble corridors *(main picture)* overlook Neptune's Courtyard. They are lined with portraits of the Grand Masters, their coats of arms and suits of armour.

3 Tapestry Chamber

In this elegant room, the senior Knights attended to day-to-day business and, in later years, the Maltese parliament met. It is now lit dimly to preserve the sumptuous Gobelin tapestries.

4 Gobelin Tapestries

Known as *Les Tentures des Indes* (the Indies Tapestries) *(below)*, for their depictions of exotic scenes, they were donated in 1710 by Grand Master Perellos.

5 Supreme Council Hall

This is the grandest room in the palace, also known as the Hall of St Michael and St George. It has glittering chandeliers, a coffered ceiling and a stunning frieze *(left)* which vividly depicts the Great Siege of 1565. The minstrel's gallery at one end of the hall once decorated the palace chapel, but came originally from the warship *Grand Carrack* in which the Knights departed from Rhodes.

6 Great Siege Frieze

This dynamic frieze *(above)* recounting the key events in the Knights' celebrated defence of the island was painted by Matteo Perez d'Aleccio (1547–1616) between 1575 and 1581.

7 Ambassador's Room

The Grand Masters used this handsome chamber *(above)* for private audiences and to impress foreign dignitaries. Matteo Perez d'Aleccio painted the frieze, which represents important moments in the history of the Order of St John.

8 State Dining Hall

Badly damaged by aerial bombardment during World War II, this beautifully proportioned chamber is lined with portraits of British monarchs and Maltese heads of state.

9 Armoury

The Palace Armoury *(above)*, located in the former stables, contains more than 5,000 pieces of military hardware. There are cannons, guns and entire walls lined with evil-looking devices for hacking, spearing and spiking your opponent.

10 Parade Armour

The highlight of the Armoury's collection is exquisitely decorated parade armour made for the Grand Masters. The most elaborate is a suit made for Grand Master Martino Garzes (1595–61), which has an intricate etched pattern.

The Maltese Cross

The eight-pointed cross, symbol of the Knights of Malta, can be found throughout the Grand Palace. It is said that the eight points symbolize the eight Beatitudes as well as the eight original *Langues* (national "tongues", or chapters) of the Order. The four arms of the cross are supposed to represent the four cardinal Virtues: Fortitude, Justice, Temperance and Perseverance. Although the cross is traditionally said to date back to the founding of the Order in the 11th century, this particular style of cross didn't come into common use until the mid-16th century.

St John's Co-Cathedral, Valletta

St John's Co-Cathedral, designed by Gerolamo Cassar and consecrated in 1578, looms over Valletta like a giant fortress. Yet when you step over the threshold, the austerity gives way to an interior of dazzling beauty. The marble floor is covered with richly inlaid tombstones, every wall is intricately carved with flowers and garlands, and the vaulted ceiling is splendidly painted with frescoes by Mattia Preti (1613–99). The Cathedral's treasures include a magnificent painting of St John the Baptist by Caravaggio as well as a series of exquisite tapestries with designs by Rubens and Poussin. Since the 1820s, it has shared cathedral status with L-Imdina's Cathedral of St Paul.

The choir

🚫 You may be refused entry if you are not dressed respectfully. Shoes with pointed or narrow heels are not allowed as they can damage the delicate floor, but protective slippers can be bought for €1.

🍴 Nearby you'll find Valletta's most venerable (but pricey) café, the Caffè Cordina (see p66) which has tables out on the square.

• Misrah San Ġwann (visitors' entrance on Triq Ir-Repubblika)
• Map H2/J2
• 2122 0536
• Open 9:30am–4pm Mon–Fri, 9:30am–12:30pm Sat
• Adm €6, seniors €4.60, students €3.50, under 12s free
• www.stjohnsco cathedral.org

Top 10 Features

1. Façade
2. Chapel of the Blessed Sacrament
3. Bell towers
4. Nave
5. Marble Tombstones
6. Chapels of the Langues
7. Oratory
8. High Altar
9. Monument of Grand Master Cotoner
10. Museum

Façade
The cathedral's severe, unadorned façade reflects its role as the centrepiece of the new fortress-city.

Chapel of the Blessed Sacrament
Adjacent to the High Altar, this chapel has been completely restored; its interior carved walls and dome (above) have been cleaned and regilded.

Bell towers
The severe bell towers flanking the main entrance (right) are the model for the twin bell towers that adorn virtually every church in Malta.

Nave
The nave (above) was at first as plain as the façade. It was transformed in the 1660s, when Mattia Preti gave it a Baroque makeover and painted his magnificent frescoes depicting episodes from the life of St John.

For more on the Order of the Knights of St John See p13

5 Marble Tombstones

The entire floor of the church is a sea of multicoloured marble, where 400 Knights are buried beneath dazzling tombstones. Each is adorned with the coat of arms of its aristocratic occupant, along with symbols reminding onlookers of the inevitability of death *(left)*.

Main entrance

6 Chapels of the Langues

Each of the *Langues* (the national chapters of the Order of St John) was given its own chapel off one of the aisles on either side of the nave. The *Langues* vied with each other to create the most lavish chapel, and all are richly decorated. Those of Provence and Italy *(above)* are the most sumptuous.

Caravaggio the Knight

When Caravaggio (1571–1610) arrived on Malta in 1607, the celebrated painter had a price on his head; he had killed a man in a street brawl the previous year. In spite of this, he impressed the Grand Master and was made a Knight. But soon after painting *The Beheading of John the Baptist* he was in trouble again; he injured another Knight and was thrown into prison. He escaped, and was stripped of his Knighthood as a "foul and rotten member".

7 Oratory

The Oratory contains Caravaggio's masterpiece and Malta's most famous work of art, *The Beheading of John the Baptist* (1608).

8 High Altar

The 17th-century High Altar *(right)* is made of gold, silver and bronze, encrusted with precious jewels in many hues.

9 Monument of Grand Master Cotoner

The gilt-bronze bust of the diplomat and strategist is carried by two slaves, who represent Asia and Africa.

10 Museum

The museum displays the co-cathedral's most important paintings, lavishly embroidered vestments, illuminated antiphonaries, silver plate and a fine collection of 17th-century tapestries.

The crypt, which houses 12 tombs of Grand Masters, is in a poor state of preservation and is rarely open to the public.

Left **Grim Reaper memorial stone** Centre **Monstrance** Right *The Beheading of John the Baptist*

🔟 Treasures of St John's Co-Cathedral

1 Grim Reaper Memorial Stone
Entering the cathedral, you can't miss the chilling depiction of the Grim Reaper, scythe aloft, which adorns the tombstone of a French Knight. The inscription reminds visitors that "You who tread on me will soon be trodden on".

2 Altarpiece of St George
The altarpiece in the Chapel of Aragon was originally Mattia Preti's calling card – he sent it to Malta as an example of his work. It led to his commission to paint the church's ceiling frescoes.

3 Embroidered Vestments
The Cathedral Museum contains ornate robes dating back to the 16th century. Most belonged to the Spanish Grand Master Nicolas Cotoner.

4 Monstrance
This flamboyant Baroque monstrance was made to hold the reliquary containing the right hand of St John the Baptist. Stolen by Napoleon, the reliquary was lost at sea.

Memorial to Nicolas Cotoner

5 The Beheading of John the Baptist (1608)
Caravaggio's emotive masterpiece depicts the very moment after the sword has dropped and St John the Baptist has fallen, bleeding, to the ground.

6 Portraits of the Grand Masters
The highlight of the painting gallery is a series of portraits by the French artist Antoine de Favray (1706–c.1791). The best is his depiction of the pleasure-loving Grand Master Pinto de Fonseca.

7 Tombs of the Grand Masters
The resplendent Chapels of the Langues contain monuments to the Grand Masters. The most lavish belong to Grand Masters Nicolas Cotoner and Ramón Perellos in the Chapel of Aragon.

8 Tapestries
Flemish tapestries, based on cartoons by Rubens and Poussin, are among the most precious objects in the Cathedral Museum. They adorn the church on special occasions, such as the Pope's visit in 1990.

9 Blessed Sacrament Gate
According to legend, this silver gate was painted black to foil Napoleon's rapacious troops. It is one of the few silver objects to survive the plunder.

10 High Altar
The High Altar (1686) is a Baroque design in gilded silver, studded with precious jewels. At the centre, a relief in gilded bronze depicts the Last Supper.

For more on the Grand Masters of the Order of the Knights of St John See pp36–7

The Knights of St John

The Order of the Knights of St John was founded in Jerusalem in the 11th century and is the oldest Order of Chivalry in existence. The Knights were required to show proof of noble birth (an ancient rule that was only modified in the 1990s) and were organized into national chapters called Langues. The supreme head is the Grand Master. After the fall of Jerusalem in the late 13th century, the Knights built an island fortress on Rhodes. In 1480, Grand Master Pierre d'Aubusson successfully defended Rhodes against an Ottoman siege. The Knights were, however, ousted by the Ottomans in 1522.

The Holy Roman Emperor Charles V offered the Knights the Maltese islands in exchange for the annual payment of a live Maltese falcon, and they arrived in Malta in 1530. They withstood the Turks during the Great Siege of 1565, built the walled city of Valletta and erected defences across the islands. During the 17th and 18th centuries, as the Ottoman threat diminished, the Order fell into decline. When Napoleon arrived on Maltese shores in 1798, the Knights submitted to the French without a fight. They were forced to leave Malta, but the Order refused to be crushed. Although still stateless today, it continues to function, focusing primarily on charitable and religious works.

Top 10 Important Dates for the Knights of St John

1. c.1100: Order founded after First Crusade.
2. 1309: Knights take island of Rhodes.
3. 1522: Ottomans oust Knights from Rhodes.
4. 1530: Knights given Malta by Charles V.
5. 1565: Knights victorious against Ottomans in first Great Siege.
6. 1571: Ottomans defeated at Battle of Lepanto.
7. 1578: St John's (later co-cathedral) consecrated.
8. 1660s: Mattia Preti transforms St John's into Baroque masterpiece.
9. 1792: Revolutionaries seize the Order's considerable French assets.
10. 1798: Knights cede Malta to Napoleon.

The First Grand Master

This coloured engraving from Father Helyot's *History and Costumes of Monastic Orders* (1842) shows Raymond de Puy, the first Grand Master. His robe is adorned with the white Maltese cross.

The Ottoman siege of Rhodes in 1480

 For more on the Maltese Cross See p9

Ħaġar Qim and Mnajdra Temples

These ancient limestone temples, built during the Ġgantija and Tarxien eras (3600–3200 and 3150–2500 BC respectively), are set on a clifftop in one of the most beautiful and unspoilt regions of Malta. Ħaġar Qim is unique and complex in design. Mnajdra, closer to the cliff edge, is even more spectacular, particularly in spring surrounded by fields of poppies. Mnajdra's astronomical alignments have led to it being called "a calendar in stone". Renovations, completed in 2009, were designed to stop further erosion of these monuments.

Gigantic Stone, Ħaġar Qim

🕐 Special early morning tours are organized by Heritage Malta four times a year (on the solstices and equinoxes) to see the first rays of the rising sun hit particular stones. Book early as there's a very long waiting list.

🍴 Refreshments are available at the visitor centre.

• Triq Ħaġar Qim, beyond Il-Qrendi
• Map C6
• 2142 4231
• Open daily 9am–4:30pm (until 6:45pm in summer)
• Adm €10 (concessions €7, children €5.50)
• www.heritagemalta.org

Top 10 Features

1. Main Entrance, Ħaġar Qim
2. Decorative Objects, Ħaġar Qim
3. Gigantic Stone, Ħaġar Qim
4. External Altar, Ħaġar Qim
5. Misqa Tanks
6. Small Temple, Mnajdra
7. Façade of South Temple, Mnajdra
8. Porthole Niche, South Temple, Mnajdra
9. Carving of Temple Façade, Central Temple, Mnajdra
10. Islet of Filfla

Decorative Objects, Ħaġar Qim
The most beautiful objects found at Ħaġar Qim are statuettes, presumed to represent deities. It is also notable for a pair of finely decorated stone altars, unique in Malta, with an elaborate pitted design.

Gigantic Stone, Ħaġar Qim
The biggest stone in the complex – technically called an "orthostat" – is just to the right of the main entrance. It measures a huge 21 sq m (220 sq ft) and weighs 20 tonnes – one of the largest found in any Maltese temple.

Main Entrance, Ħaġar Qim
Ħaġar Qim's dramatic main entrance *(below)* remains surprisingly intact, its large honey-coloured stones neatly interlocking.

External Altar, Ħaġar Qim
Just beyond the gigantic stone is an exterior shrine and oracle hole *(left)*. It has been suggested that the central column and tapered block are male and female fertility symbols.

Misqa Tanks
A natural trail leading off the main passage will take you to a hill. It is pocked with bell-shaped water tanks, probably carved out of the rock in order to provide the nearby temples with water.

Statues found at the temples and many other key artifacts are held at the National Museum of Archaeology, Valletta See p40

Mnajdra

6 Small Temple, Mnajdra

Almost nothing survives of Mnajdra's oldest temple *(above)*, which dates from the Ggantija era *(see p35)*. One of the oldest free-standing monuments, its pitted decorations may be a tally for the rising of particular constellations.

Ħaġar Qim

7 Façade of South Temple, Mnajdra

The South Temple is one of the best preserved in all Malta. The façade *(below)* has a long exterior bench; it may be that outdoor rituals took place in the courtyard in front.

8 Porthole Niche, South Temple, Mnajdra

The porthole niche is one of the finest pieces of original stonework still *in situ* in Malta's temples. It is framed by three stones with pitted designs.

10 Islet of Filfla

This tiny offshore islet *(above)* is now a wildlife reserve, but it retains its ancient mystique. It may have had special ritual significance for the temple-builders.

9 Carving of Temple Façade, Central Temple, Mnajdra

The most recent of the three, the Central Temple was built between the two existing temples. One of its huge orthostats shows a carved representation of a temple façade *(below)* – perhaps an early architectural design.

A Stone Calendar

Mnajdra's South Temple displays an extraordinary astronomical alignment. At the equinoxes (21 Mar and 23 Sep), sunlight shines directly through the main doorway. At the summer solstice (21 Jun), the rays fall on the big stone to the left of the doorway, at the winter solstice (22 Dec), on the corresponding right-hand stone.

For more Maltese temples and ancient sites See pp34–5

⭑10 L-Imdina and Ir-Rabat

L-Imdina is Malta's most hauntingly beautiful city. It and neighbouring Ir-Rabat were once part of the same settlement, but the Arabs walled off L-Imdina and made it a fortress-city. Still caught within the impregnable walls, it has barely changed in centuries, and the elegant palaces are still home to ancient Maltese families. L-Imdina remains a tiny time capsule of a city, but Ir-Rabat, which spreads beyond the walls, has grown into a more workaday town. Nonetheless, it boasts some important Christian sights, from the cave where St Paul is said to have lived to early Christian catacombs and mesmerizing medieval frescoes.

L-Imdina

🎧 A fascinating audio-guide is available at St Paul's Catacombs.

☕ Visit the Fontanella Tea Gardens *(see p89)* for a restorative coffee and delicious cakes.

- Map C4
- St Paul's Cathedral: Pjazza San Pawl. 2145 6620. Open Mon–Sat. Free
- Cathedral Museum: Pjazza Ta' L-Arcisqof. 2145 4697. Open Mon–Sat. Adm €5
- Palazzo Vilhena: Pjazza San Publiju. 2145 5951. Open daily. Adm €5
- The Mdina Experience: Pjazza Mesquita. 2145 4322. Open daily. Adm €6
- Domus Romana: Il-Wesgħa Tal-Mużew. 2145 4125. Open daily. Adm €6 (children €3)
- St Paul's Church: Misrah Il-Parocċa. Open Mon–Sat. Free
- St Paul's Catacombs: Triq Sant'Agatha. 2145 4526. Open daily. Adm €4
- St Agatha's Catacombs: Triq Sant' Agata. 2145 4419. Open Mon–Sat. Adm €5

Top 10 Features

1. St Paul's Cathedral, L-Imdina
2. Cathedral Museum, L-Imdina
3. Palazzo Vilhena, L-Imdina
4. Triq Villegaignon, L-Imdina
5. Walls and Gates, L-Imdina
6. The Mdina Experience
7. Domus Romana, Ir-Rabat
8. St Paul's Church and Grotto, Ir-Rabat
9. St Paul's Catacombs, Ir-Rabat
10. St Agatha's Catacombs, Ir-Rabat

St Paul's Cathedral, L-Imdina

Lorenzo Gafa's handsome Baroque cathedral *(above)* is topped by an elegant dome. The marble tomb-stones laid into the floor are dedicated to notable prelates.

Cathedral Museum, L-Imdina

Housed in a faded Baroque building with a sweeping marble staircase, the museum is charming, quirky and old-fashioned. The highlight is a series of Dürer woodcuts.

Palazzo Vilhena, L-Imdina

Grand Master Vilhena commissioned Guion de Mondion, architect of the Manoel Theatre, to build this lavish Baroque palace in 1725. Most of its opulent decoration was stripped away in later years, when it became a hospital. The building now houses the Natural History Museum *(left)* in its old wards.

St Paul's Cathedral shares "Co-Cathedral" status with St John's, Valletta.

4 Triq Villegaignon, L-Imdina

L-Imdina's main street (left) is lined with the city's oldest and most beautiful palaces, many still occupied by noble families. The finest is the Palazzo Falson (Norman House), partly from the 13th century and now an excellent museum.

5 Walls and Gates, L-Imdina

The imposing city walls were first built by the Arabs. The lavish Baroque main gate (left) was constructed in 1724, and later restored. The beautiful gardens below enhance the visual appeal of the area.

6 The Mdina Experience

The best of L-Imdina's audiovisual attractions, this offers a good whistle-stop introduction to the city's history.

7 Domus Romana, Ir-Rabat

On the outskirts of Ir-Rabat, near L-Imdina's Greek Gate, this consists of a small museum and the time-worn ruins of an opulent Roman town house. The museum contains some wonderful mosaics and sculptures (left).

8 St Paul's Church and Grotto, Ir-Rabat

St Paul is said to have lived in this grotto during his stay in Malta, and the cave remains a place of pilgrimage. The church (below) that protects the grotto is gloomy and dull, but it contains a statue of the Madonna said to have miraculous powers.

9 St Paul's Catacombs, Ir-Rabat

These fascinating Phoenician catacombs, a handful of which have their original decoration, were later used by early Christians.

10 St Agatha's Catacombs, Ir-Rabat

St Agatha is said to have prayed here. The main chapel (left) is beautifully decorated with medieval frescoes. Half-lost within the catacombs is another, exquisitely painted chapel from the 4th century AD.

St Agatha

St Paul is the most important saint in Malta, but St Agatha comes a close second. According to legend, the beautiful young virgin Agatha, a native of Sicily, caught the eye of the Roman governor but refused his advances. She fled to Malta to escape persecution. She is said to have prayed in a small cave in Ir-Rabat, and an underground chapel was later built there in her memory. After a few months (some say years) she returned to Sicily and was then captured by the Roman governor, who had her tortured and killed.

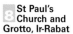

Joint tickets for Domus Romana, St Paul's Catacombs and Palazzo Vilhena are available (adults €12, concessions €9 and children €6).

17

Palazzo Parisio, In-Naxxar

The Palazzo Parisio was originally built in 1733 for Portuguese Grand Master Manoel de Vilhena. In 1898 it was bought by the Marquis Giuseppe Scicluna, who transformed it into one of the island's most extravagantly beautiful residences. The Marquis commissioned the finest Maltese and Italian craftsmen to embellish his palace, filled it with exquisite furnishings and works of art, and introduced modern amenities such as electric light and telephones (Malta's first). Sadly, the Marquis died only a year after the palace's transformation was complete. It remains in the hands of the Scicluna family and the house, along with its glorious Baroque gardens, are now open to the public.

The Music Room

🕐 If you aren't in the mood to explore the palace, it's possible to purchase a ticket just for the gardens.

🍴 Caffè Luna, the palace's restaurant, serves excellent food. It is open 9am–6pm for breakfast, lunch, teas and coffees.

- *Pjazza Vittorja, In-Naxxar*
- *Map C4*
- *2141 2461*
- *Open 9am–6pm Mon–Sat (last admission 5:30pm; audio-guides available; guided tours on the hour Mon–Fri (last tour 1pm). For private guided tours call in advance*
- *Adm €12 (concessions €7, children €5) Gardens only: €6 (concessions €4.50)*
- *www.palazzoparisio. com*

Top 10 Features

1. Façade
2. Entrance Hall
3. Marble Staircase
4. Dining Room
5. Main Bedroom
6. Study/Library
7. Music Room
8. Ballroom
9. Billiard Room
10. Gardens

Façade
The elegant façade of the palace *(below)* is, sadly, hard to appreciate since it fronts a main road. It overlooks In-Naxxar's central square, dominated by a flamboyant Baroque church.

Entrance Hall
Opulence envelops you as soon as you enter. The vestibule is flamboyantly decorated in the Pompeii Style with classical statues and a frescoed ceiling.

Marble Staircase
The coping over the magnificent staircase *(right)* is formed by a single piece of gleaming white Carrara marble 6 m (20 ft) in length.

Dining Room
The dining room *(above)* is decorated in the Pompeii Style popular around 1900. The huge dining table is laid with special Royal Doulton china and glittering crystal.

There's another Palazzo Parisio in Valletta; it achieved notoriety as Napoleon's headquarters during his brief visit in 1798. See p33

Main Bedroom

Sumptuously decorated in pale green and gold, the bedroom *(right)* boasts hand-painted walls topped with a delicate fringe of green and gold made of stucco. Off the bedroom is the family chapel and a pretty ladies' dressing room with gilded furniture.

Study/Library

With its brocaded curtains and Art Nouveau chairs, this room *(below)* has a decidedly French feel. Stucco reliefs show plump cherubs equipped with a telephone.

Music Room

This beautiful little salon has walls of fine silk and an extravagantly gilded ceiling. Each item of furniture features a different musical instrument. The Maltese cross has been incorporated into the design of the inlaid floor.

Ballroom

The opulent Ballroom *(right)* is a magnificent golden whirl. Vast chandeliers are reflected in enormous gilt mirrors, and the ceiling is covered with elaborate stucco.

Billiard Room

This room still contains the original, enormous billiard table sent over from London. The walls and 3-D "carved" ceiling are a triumph of *trompe l'oeil*.

Gardens

The palace's beautiful gardens are loveliest, and fragrant with orange and lemon blossom, in spring. There are two formal gardens and an Orangerie with a 17th-century grotto.

The Palazzo in the Movies

This opulent stately home is much in demand today as a film and television location. It has doubled as a French château for the 2002 movie *The Count of Monte Cristo*, as a Genoa hotel in the BBC dramatization of *Daniel Deronda* (2002) and as an Italian villa in another BBC television drama, *Byron* (2003).

🔟 Marsaxlokk

This enchanting fishing village is set around an azure bay. Traditional fishing boats painted in bright colours bob in the harbour, and the quays are spread with brilliantly coloured fishing nets. Life continues much as it has for decades, if not centuries, in this small and tight-knit community, which has somehow survived the daily deluge of tourists without selling its soul. The modern era has left some ugly marks, however: the power station out on Delimara Point blights the view, as does the enormous container port around the headland. For now at least, Marsaxlokk's sleepy charms remain intact.

Delimara Point

🅖 Book early for Sunday lunch, as many Maltese families like to get together in the pretty seafront town for long lunches.

🅠 There are numerous dining options all along the seafront. Try Ir-Rizzu or Is-Sajjied *(see p97)*.

• Map E5

Top 10 Features

1. Luzzus
2. Quays
3. Daily Market
4. Sunday Fish Market
5. Church of Our Lady of Pompeii
6. Fish Restaurants
7. "Seasick Summit" Monument
8. St Lucian's Tower
9. Delimara Point
10. St Peter's Pool

1 Luzzus

These traditional brightly painted boats *(right)* are said to owe their design to the ancient Phoenicians, who first arrived in Malta around 800 BC. The Eye of Osiris, an ancient symbol of protection against evil, is still painted on every prow.

2 Quays

The picturesque harbour of Marsaxlokk is hemmed in by quays strewn with brilliantly coloured fishing nets of cobalt blue and emerald green. The local fishermen are usually hard at work fixing boats *(above)* or mending nets.

3 Daily Market

A section of the quays is dedicated to a daily market *(below)*, where all kinds of clothes, souvenirs, CDs and sunglasses are sold. On Sundays, the tourist tat makes way for fresh fish.

4 Sunday Fish Market

Marsaxlokk's fish market *(left)* is a local legend. Locals and tourists alike come to gawp at the array of fabulous fresh produce on the seafront stalls. If buying fish, look for bright eyes and red gills.

5 Church of Our Lady of Pompeii

This pretty little church *(below)* sits just back from the harbour. As in many Maltese churches, it has two clocks – one painted and permanently set at a few moments before the witching hour of midnight to ward off evil spirits.

6 Fish Restaurants

Many of the old fishermen's houses that surround the quays *(below)* have been converted into fish restaurants. A long, lazy seafood lunch after a visit to the fish market is a Sunday tradition.

8 St Lucian's Tower

This squat little fortress *(below)* guards the headland beyond Marsaxlokk. It was erected by the Knights in 1610 as part of their coastal defences. Now it houses the Malta Centre for Fisheries Sciences (not open to the public).

7 "Seasick Summit" Monument

A monument on the coast road from Marsaxlokk to Birżebbuġa commemorates the historic meeting of Mikhail Gorbachev and George Bush Sr on board a cruiser in Marsaxlokk Bay in 1989; this marked the beginning of the end of the Cold War.

The "Seasick Summit"

In December 1989, Mikhail Gorbachev and George Bush Sr declared an end to the Cold War after two days of talks aboard a cruiser moored in Marsaxlokk Bay. Unfortunately, the summit coincided with some of the worst storms ever to hit the Maltese coast. The flotilla out in the bay was badly battered, and the Press nicknamed the meeting the "Seasick Summit".

9 Delimara Point

This long finger of land sticks into the sea beyond Marsaxlokk harbour. It is quiet and rural, with tiny bays, fields, wonderful walks – and a power plant.

10 St Peter's Pool

The closest swimming hole to Marsaxlokk, this *(left)* is hidden away on the eastern side of Delimara Point. Fishing boats may be able to take you there if you don't have your own transport.

Malta's Top 10

TOP 10 Ħal-Saflieni Hypogeum, Paola

This vast underground necropolis is quite simply one of the most extraordinary archaeological sites in the world. The upper level dates back to around 3600 BC, and two more levels were subsequently dug below. The stunning chambers, carved with incredible delicacy and refinement, echo the forms of the above-ground temples found across the islands. Around 7,000 bodies were found here, deposited over a period of a thousand years. This suggests that only certain members of society were eligible for burial here – but, like so much else relating to Malta's prehistoric temple-building culture, there are more questions than answers.

Oracle Chamber

🟢 Book weeks in advance; only 80 people are allowed to visit the Hypogeum daily and there is a long waiting list. Note that there is no admission for children under six years of age.

🟠 There is nowhere to eat well in Paola but the waterfront in Birgu is close by and boasts a few restaurants *(see p74).*

Triq Ic-Ċimiterju
• Map E5
• 2180 5019
• Open daily 9am–4pm
• Adm €30 (concessions €15, children €12)
• Advance booking essential
• Photography not allowed
• http://booking. heritagemalta.org/ (bookings); www. heritagemalta.com (information)

Top 10 Features

1. Entrance Trilithon
2. Upper Level (3600–3300 BC)
3. Middle Level (3300–3000 BC)
4. Lower Level (3000–2400 BC)
5. Oracle Chamber
6. Holy of Holies
7. Main Chamber
8. Rock-cut Pit
9. Sleeping Lady
10. Recovered Artifacts

1 Entrance Trilithon

Some constructions in the upper level of the Hypogeum were destroyed by builders in the early 1900s. But the entrance doorway, in the typical trilithon form of two large stones supporting a lintel, has survived intact.

2 Upper Level (3600–3300 BC)

The upper level is the oldest section of the Hypogeum and it is apparent that the temple-builders originally enlarged a natural cave. This is the only level of the necropolis in which some ancient bones have been left *in situ.*

3 Middle Level (3300–3000 BC)

The most important chambers – and the most accomplished examples of stone-carving and decoration – are found on this level.

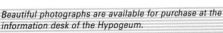

Beautiful photographs are available for purchase at the information desk of the Hypogeum.

4 Lower Level (3000–2400 BC)

The lower level *(right)* is reached via a series of uneven steps. These lead to a series of chambers separated by walls about 2m (6ft) in height, making movement from one room to the next difficult.

Entrance Trilithon

5 Oracle Chamber

Red-ochre swirls decorate the ceiling of this extraordinary chamber. A niche carved into the wall can be used to great theatrical effect; it allows low-pitched (usually male) voices to reverberate impressively around the chamber.

6 Holy of Holies

This is easily the most impressive of all the chambers in the Hypogeum, entered through a magnificently carved monumental façade featuring a fine trilithon doorway. This entrance echoes those of temples found above ground, but is here carved into the rock.

Entrance to lower level

Key

Upper Level
Middle Level
Lower Level

9 Sleeping Lady

This is the most beautiful of all the statues found in Malta's ancient temples. The enormously plump woman dreams serenely. Perhaps she symbolizes death – or is a priestess in a trance.

7 Main Chamber

A series of recesses are set into the curved walls of the main chamber *(above)*. Their function remains unclear. Perhaps statues were placed here, or perhaps the dead were left here before finally being buried elsewhere.

8 Rock-cut Pit

Just off the main chamber is a small cavern, sometimes known as the "snake pit" or "votive pit". It has been thought that the area was used for holding animals before they were sacrificed. The famous statue of the *Sleeping Lady* was found here.

10 Recovered Artifacts

The many artifacts found in the Hypogeum include amulets, figurines and vases. One of the most curious is a headless statue. It was found with two limestone heads, one of which fits perfectly.

The Hypogeum and the Xagħra Circle

The Hypogeum was first excavated in the early 1900s using rudimentary archaeological techniques, and most of the early notes were subsequently lost. The absence of any information from the opening of this unique site was a huge blow to modern archaeologists, but the discovery of the Xagħra Circle in Gozo (another underground necropolis long thought lost) has given them fresh hope. The Xagħra Circle has been excavated, and the new information it has provided has improved our understanding of the Hypogeum.

The Hypogeum's function remains mysterious; some eccentrics have contended that it was a control centre for alien spaceships.

🔟 The Citadel, Ir-Rabat/Victoria, Gozo

All roads in Gozo lead to Victoria – or Ir-Rabat to locals. The Gozitan capital is crowned by the walled Citadel, the hilltop city whose handsome silhouette is visible from almost everywhere on the island. For many years, the island of Gozo was plagued by raiding corsairs and Saracens, who took the people into slavery. Life was so dangerous that, right up until 1673, the population was required by law, for their own safety, to spend every night within the Citadel. Now rather charmingly run-down, the Citadel offers magnificent views, a fine cathedral and a clutch of fascinating museums.

The Citadel, Ir-Rabat/Victoria

☕ The Citadel Card offers admission to four museums for €8. Audio-guides can be picked up at the Cathedral ticket office.

🍴 Ta' Rikardu *(see p103)* is a popular choice for a snack.

• Map D2
• Cathedral: Pjazza Katidral. 2155 4101. Open Mon–Sat. Free
• Cathedral Museum: Triq Il-Fosos. 2155 6087. Open daily. Adm €5.50
• Museum of Archaeology: Triq Bieb L-Imdina. 2155 6144. Open daily. Adm €3
• Old Prison: Triq Il-Fosos. 2156 5988. Open daily. Adm €3
• Folklore Museum: Triq Bernardo DeOpuo. 2156 2034. Open daily. Adm €3
• Gozo Nature Museum: Triq Il-Kwartier San Martin. 2155 6153. Open daily. Adm €3
• Gozo Crafts Centre: Triq Bieb L-Imdina. 2155 6160. Open daily. Free

Top 10 Features

1. Walls
2. Cathedral
3. Cathedral Museum
4. Museum of Archaeology
5. City Gate
6. Folklore Museum
7. Old Prison
8. Norman Ruins
9. Gozo Nature Museum
10. Gozo Crafts Centre

Walls
The Citadel's sturdy walls *(above)* owe their appearance to the Knights, who had them substantially reinforced after their victory over the Turks in 1565. Although the Turkish threat had been quelled, the Knights feared vengeance.

Cathedral
The lavish Baroque cathedral *(main image)* was designed by the renowned Lorenzo Gafa and completed in 1716. It is only the latest place of worship on this site; a megalithic temple is thought to have occupied the hilltop 7,000 years ago.

Cathedral Museum
The Cathedral Museum *(below)* contains some eccentric items – like the stole of El Salvadorean Archbishop Oscar Romero, assassinated in 1980 while saying Mass.

The Citadel's museums are open from 9am–5pm. Last admission is at 4:30pm.

Museum of Archaeology

Housed in the elegant Casa Bondi, this museum contains wonderful artifacts from Ġgantija, Xagħra Circle and other Gozitan sites. Look out for the beautiful "shaman's bundle" *(above)*.

City Gate

The main city gate is very plain, it was punched through the walls in the 1950s to allow the statue of Santa Marija from the Cathedral to pass. The original city gate is nearby.

Folklore Museum

Three adjoining period houses host this intriguing museum. Displays of rural Gozitan life include reconstructions of typical homes, a grain mill *(below)* and tools for various crafts.

Norman Ruins

Much of the northern part of the Citadel consists of ruined houses, walls and streets, which in many cases have been reduced to rubble. Many date back to the 12th century; EU funds are being sought for reconstruction.

Gozo Nature Museum

This small museum, located in a 17th-century inn, has rather dull exhibits related to Gozo's wildlife *(right)*, geography and geology. Pride of place goes to a fragment of moon rock, which was donated to the Maltese people by US President Richard Nixon.

Gozo Crafts Centre

A good place to get an overview of local crafts, particularly lace-making and silk, cotton and wool weaving. Cosy woven rugs, sweaters and other items are usually available to buy.

Old Prison

This was in use from the mid-16th to the 20th centuries. The cells and corridors are still etched with prisoners' graffiti *(above)*, including a rendition of a galley with its oars. As a young man, Grand Master de la Vallette was imprisoned here after a brawl.

Dragut Rias and the Raid of 1551

Gozo, hard to defend and vulnerable to attack, suffered countless raids by pirates and corsairs. The worst occurred in 1551, when legendary corsair Dragut Rias attacked the Citadel and took nearly 6,000 people into slavery – virtually the entire population of the island. A local soldier, Bernardo DeOpuo, found the thought of his wife and daughters being sold into slavery so intolerable that he slit their throats rather than allow their capture. A street in the Citadel is named after him.

Dwejra, Gozo

The western tip of Gozo is savagely beautiful, with wild, wave-battered cliffs, dramatic rock formations and wind-whipped headlands. This stretch of coastline, known as Dwejra, is blessed with celebrated natural landmarks such as Fungus Rock and the stunning Azure Window – possibly the most photographed sight in Gozo. The area is considered one of the finest in the Mediterranean for diving and snorkelling, and the cliffs are etched with walking paths offering panoramic views. In summer the sea is a calm and perfect blue, but in winter huge waves dash dramatically against the cliffs.

Dwejra Point

🌀 Visit at dusk if possible; a Dwejra sunset is unforgettable.

🍴 Enjoy a picnic by the seashore or savour restaurant dishes on your way to the inland sea.

• Map C1

Top 10 Features

1. Dwejra Point
2. Azure Window
3. Inland Sea
4. Fungus Rock
5. Blue Hole
6. Qawra Tower
7. Dwejra Bay
8. Chapel of St Anne
9. Boat Trips
10. Wildlife

Dwejra Point
1 This mighty promontory is the most westerly point of Gozo's dramatic coast. It is pierced by the Azure Window. Daring visitors walk out to the farthest tip for spectacular views – and sheer drops on either side.

Fungus Rock
4 The strange, squat rock *(above)* in Dwejra Bay gets its name from a rare plant, *Cynomorium coccineum*, that still grows copiously there. The Knights prized the "fungus" highly: anyone caught stealing it was sentenced to three years in the galleys. The rock remains out of bounds to this day.

Azure Window
2 This huge arch of rock *(above)* nearly 100 m (328 ft) high is perhaps the most spectacular natural phenomenon in the Maltese islands.

Inland Sea
3 This shallow lagoon *(below)* is a popular spot for a swim, although it's really more of a pond than a "sea". Boats take visitors in through a passage in the rocks.

The area around Dwejra has no sandy beaches but several good sites for swimming, diving and snorkelling **See pp50–51**

Blue Hole
The Blue Hole *(right)* is another remarkable natural phenomenon close to the Azure Window: a chimney, about 10 m (33 ft) wide and 25 m (82 ft) long, which links the open sea with the Inland Sea through an underwater arch. It's an extremely popular dive site.

Qawra Tower
This squat little tower *(below)* was erected by the Knights in the 16th century to guard the precious "fungus" that covered Fungus Rock. A hoist was built to winch an official plant-gatherer across to the Rock, which was difficult to scale.

The General's Root
Fungus Rock is known in Maltese as "The General's Rock", after the General of the Galleys who discovered the rank-smelling plant that grows there. The "General's Root", as the plant became known, was thought to cure dysentery, staunch bleeding, and prevent infection in wounds, and the Rock was kept under constant watch to deter thieves. Modern tests have shown the plant to have no medicinal value whatsoever; the Rock is still protected, but purely for reasons of conservation.

Dwejra Bay
The sweeping bay that curves around Fungus Rock is the best place for swimming as the shallow rocks offer easy access to the water. It's also a popular yacht anchorage.

Chapel of St Anne
This simple little chapel overlooks the Inland Sea. Built in 1963 on the site of a much older church, it is rather dishevelled but important for local people.

Boat Trips
Fishermen run trips *(right)* from the Inland Sea to the Azure Window through a curious rift in the cliff. The journey is short but exhilarating.

Wildlife
Despite illegal hunting and trapping, the Dwejra cliffs remain an important bird breeding and nesting site. As well as the "Malta Fungus", Fungus Rock is home to the rare Maltese wall lizard.

TOP10 Comino

Comino is a diminutive but paradisiacal island with a permanent population of just four or five. The Romans introduced the cumin that gives Comino its name, and its spicy scent, mingled with thyme and other aromatic herbs, lingers headily in the air. It takes just a couple of hours to make a circuit of the island, taking in dramatic cliffs and rocky coves where other visitors – even in the height of summer – rarely penetrate. Comino's most famous natural attraction is the dazzling Blue Lagoon; it's best to stay overnight in the island's one hotel if you want to enjoy its turquoise waters in peace.

St Niklaw Bay

🚤 Boats ferry passengers between Ċirkewwa (on Malta) and L-Imġarr (on Gozo) all year round; the trip takes around 25 minutes and the standard fare is €4.65. The Comino Hotel *(see p114)* also runs a ferry service for its guests, which non-residents can use for a fee of €10 per person from March to October.

🍴 The Comino Hotel has a restaurant and there are mobile snack vans, but the best option is to bring a picnic.

• Map A1

Top 10 Features

1. Blue Lagoon
2. St Mary's Battery
3. Chapel of Our Lady's Return from Egypt
4. The Village
5. St Mary's Tower
6. St Niklaw Bay
7. Santa Marija Bay
8. Crystal Lagoon
9. Cominotto
10. Wildlife

1 Blue Lagoon

This glorious natural inlet *(below)* divides Comino from the miniature islet of Cominotto. Its famously clear azure waters are quiet and sheltered, making them popular with families. The Lagoon has no sandy beach, but the smooth, flat rocks are inviting.

2 St Mary's Battery

This sturdy battery was built by the Knights in 1714 as part of a chain of coastal defences across the Maltese islands. It was topped with a semi-circular gun platform, but the cannons mounted there were never fired. It is now used as a lookout to protect migratory birds.

3 Chapel of Our Lady's Return from Egypt

This charming chapel *(above)* overlooking Santa Marija Bay is also called the Chapel of the Annunciation. Built in the 13th-century, its simple bell tower and whitewashed walls are reminiscent of Greek island chapels.

4 The Village

A rather ramshackle building behind St Mary's Tower, this was an isolation hospital in the early 20th century. It houses Comino's few remaining inhabitants.

Comino's single policeman runs up the flag on the little pink police station when he is in residence.

St Mary's Tower
5 The most imposing building on Comino is a crenellated watchtower *(above)* guarding the sea passage between Malta and Gozo. It was erected in 1618 by order of Grand Master Alof de Wignacourt.

St Niklaw Bay
6 This pretty bay is one of only two sandy beaches on Comino, but non-guests at the Comino Hotel must pay a fee to use it.

Santa Marija Bay
7 Comino's second sandy beach *(above)* is overlooked by a few pink bungalows, a pink police station and a whitewashed chapel. It's perfect for swimming and snorkelling.

Cominotto
9 Cominotto *(above)*, or Cominetto, is a tiny islet facing Comino across the Blue Lagoon. It has a tiny stretch of beach (at low tide you can wade across from Comino), and its rocky coastline is riddled with numerous caves. It's one of the best diving spots in the area.

Crystal Lagoon
8 Just beyond the Blue Lagoon, this natural inlet *(below)* is fringed by steep cliffs. As a result it can only be accessed by boat. The incredibly clear waters make it a popular snorkelling site.

Wildlife
10 Hunting here is illegal, but the ban is regularly violated. In spite of this, Comino offers good bird-watching opportunities, particularly in spring. For such a dry island there is diverse plant life *(left)*.

The Spanish Messiah

The great dream of the Spanish Jew Abraham ben Samuel Abulafia (1240–c.1292) was to create a new religion that would unify Jews, Christians and Muslims. Most people thought he was, at best, insane or, at worst, a heretic. He travelled to Rome, hoping to convert Pope Nicholas III – who died of apoplexy before carrying out his threat to burn Abraham at the stake. After this escape and a spell in Sicily, Abraham withdrew to a cave on the uninhabited island of Comino for three years. He wrote two texts setting out his ideas, but little is known of his later years.

Malta's Top 10

Left **Ħaġar Qim Temple** Right **"Drinking Doves" mosaic, Domus Romana, Ir-Rabat**

🔟 Moments in History

1 Prehistoric Malta (5000 BC–2500 BC)

Human settlement in Malta dates back at least to 5200 BC, although evidence found in the Għar Dalam cave has raised the possibility that it may have begun as early as 7200 BC. The first of the islands' great temples were built around 3600 BC – a thousand years before the first pyramid in Egypt. The temple period came to an abrupt and mysterious end in 2500 BC.

2 Phoenicians, Carthaginians and Romans (800 BC–AD 4th century)

Little is known of the civilization that occupied the islands from the end of the temple period until the arrival of the Phoenicians in around 800 BC. The Carthaginians used the islands as a military base from the 6th century BC, until their defeat by the Romans in 218 BC. According to legend, St Paul was shipwrecked on Malta in AD 60, initiating the country's long history of religious devotion.

3 Byzantine and Muslim Eras (AD 4th century–1090)

After the division of the Roman Empire in 395, Malta came under the control of the Byzantines until their defeat by the Arab caliphs. The Arabs left their mark both on agriculture and on the language. The islands fell to Roger I, the Norman Count, in 1090.

4 Medieval Malta (1090–1282)

The Maltese enjoyed relative independence under Norman rule, and most continued to practise Islam. In 1194, control of the islands passed to the Swabian kings, who expelled the Muslims for ever. After a brief period of French rule, Malta was acquired by Spain in 1282.

5 Spanish Rule (1282–1530)

Under the Aragonese and later the Castilians, the first local governing body, the Università, was created and the first Maltese nobles were appointed. Charles V gave the islands to the Knights of St John in 1530.

6 Knights of Malta (1530–1798)

The Knights built Valletta, along with many palaces, fortifications, and engineering works like the Wignacourt Aqueduct. They defeated the Turks in the Great Siege of 1565, a fatal blow to Muslim aims in the central Mediterranean.

The Great Siege of 1565

Preceding pages **Sunbathers on the beach at Golden Bay**

7 French Rule (1798–1800)

In 1798, Napoleon took Malta from the Knights without a struggle. He stayed just six days, but stripped the islands bare of all valuables. The outraged Maltese revolted and sought British help. The French were defeated and the British took control.

8 British Rule (1814–1939)

After defeating the French, the British declared Malta a colony in 1814 at the Treaty of Paris. It grew wealthy as an important refuelling station for British steamships on their way to India. In World War I, Malta was used as a vast hospital.

Victory St, L-Isla, 4 July 1942

9 World War II (1939–1945)

During World War II, Malta became the most bombed place on earth – 6,700 tons fell in just six weeks. The brave Maltese were awarded the George Cross in 1942 ".. to bear witness to a heroism and devotion that will long be famous in history".

10 Post-war Malta (1945–present)

Much of Malta lay in ruins after the war, although the British gave funds for reconstruction. The yearning for independence grew stronger and was finally granted in 1964. In 1979, the last British forces left the islands. Malta joined the EU in 2004.

Top 10 World War II Sites

1 Siege Bell Monument, Valletta
At the tip of Valletta, this huge bell commemorates victims of 1942's Second Great Siege.

2 Unexploded Bomb, Mosta Dome
In the dome is a replica of the bomb that pierced the roof during Mass, but miraculously failed to explode (see p38).

3 War Memorial, Floriana
This monument is inscribed with the names of 2,297 British Commonwealth servicemen.

4 George Cross Medal, National War Museum, Valletta
In 1942, the George Cross was awarded to the Maltese people for their heroism.

5 Lascaris War Rooms, Valletta
The defence of Malta and the invasion of Sicily were planned in these rooms (see p40).

6 "Faith" biplane, National War Museum, Valletta
Of three old biplanes, "Faith", "Hope" and "Charity", only Faith survived the war.

7 Malta At War Museum, Il-Birgu
This interesting little museum has re-created wartime rooms and displays period objects.

8 Red Tower, Marfa Ridge
This 17th-century fortress was used as a signalling station by the British.

9 Luqa airport, Hal Luqa
Malta's airport was an Air Force base; its unusually long runway served supply planes.

10 Dockyard Creek, Il-Birgu
HMS Illustrious, a symbol of bravery to the suffering Maltese, was moored here.

Left **Decorated stones, Tarxien** Centre **Għar Dalam Cave** Right **Cart ruts, "Clapham Junction"**

Temples and Ancient Sites

1 Mnajdra, Il-Qrendi
Mnajdra, of all the temples, most captivates visitors, thanks partly to its breathtaking clifftop setting. Its alignment has caused it to be described as a "calendar in stone" *(see pp14–15)*.

2 Ħaġar Qim, Il-Qrendi
Like nearby Mnajdra, Ħaġar Qim sits on a clifftop. A remarkable cache of "Fat Lady" (goddess) figures was found here, plus a fine altar *(see pp14–15)*.

Stone altar, Ħaġar Qim

3 Hal Saflieni Hypogeum, Paola
One of Europe's most extraordinary prehistoric sites, Hal Salflieni is a vast underground burial complex carved from solid rock *(see pp22–3)*.

4 Tarxien Temples, Paola
The largest and one of the latest temple complexes on the islands, this was built between 3600 and 2500 BC. Decorative finds include huge "Fat Ladies" and complex reliefs. An altar containing a flint knife and animal bones suggests that animals were sacrificed. Heritage Malta are working to improve accessibility and protect the remains. Ⓢ *Triq It-Tempji Neolitiċi • Map E5 • 2169 5578 • Open daily 9am–4:30pm • Adm charge • www.heritagemalta.org*

5 Ta' Ħaġrat, L-Imġarr
Two temples form this small complex. The larger, built between 3600 and 3000 BC, is one of the earliest on the islands, while the smaller dates from 3300–3000 BC. The view of L-Imġarr rising behind the temple ruins is charming. Ⓢ *Triq San Pietru • Map B4 • 2158 6264 • Open Tue, Thu, Sat 9am–noon • Adm charge • www.heritagemalta.org*

6 Skorba, Żebbiegħ
This small temple complex is, with Ġgantija in Gozo, one of the oldest free standing monuments in the world. First excavated in the 1960s, the site was undisturbed by earlier, less careful explorations. It was built on an even older village site; very early depictions of the human figure, now in Valletta's Museum of Archaeology *(see p40)*, were found here. Ⓢ *Near L-Imġarr • Map B3 • 2158 0590 • Open Tue, Thu, Sat 9am–noon • Adm charge • www.heritagemalta.org*

Mnajdra

For more on Malta's megalithic temples visit http://web.infinito.it/utenti/m/malta_mega_temples

7 Ġgantija, Ix-Xagħra, Gozo

This is one of the best-preserved Neolithic sites on the islands, in a wonderful setting overlooking Gozo's central plateau. The two temples, side by side, share the same façade. They were built around 3600 BC.
Ⓢ Triq Parisot • Map E1 • 2155 3194
• Open daily 9am–4:30pm • Adm charge
• www.heritagemalta.org

8 Xagħra Circle, Gozo

This underground burial site, undisturbed by earlier excavators, is today providing extraordinary new data. Rare but remarkably well-preserved human remains have been discovered, including a puppy with two children, and a new born baby in the arms of its mother. Ⓢ Map E1 • Not open to public
• www.heritagemalta.org

9 "Clapham Junction"

Curious grooves, or "cart ruts", etched into the limestone can be found across Malta. They have never been fully explained, but probably relate to some form of transport. The sheer number of ruts here earned it the nickname "Clapham Junction", after a famously busy London train station (see also p88). Ⓢ Near Buskett Woods • Map B5 • 24-hour access • Free • www.heritagemalta.org

10 Għar Dalam Cave and Museum, Birżebbuġa

When Malta was cut off by rising sea levels at the end of the Ice Age, animals adapted to restricted surroundings by evolving smaller forms. The bones of dwarf hippopotamuses and elephants were found here – plus evidence of Malta's earliest human settlement, dating back over 7,000 years. Ⓢ Triq Żejtun • Map E6 • 2165 7419 • Open 9am–4:30pm Mon–Sun
• Adm charge • www.heritagemalta.org

Top 10 Archeological Finds

1 "Sleeping Lady"

This exquisite statue of a sleeping woman was carved around 3000 BC. It was found in the Ħal Saflieni Hypogeum.

2 Maltese Venus

Unlike the stylized "Fat Ladies" from many temples, the Maltese Venus of Ħaġar Qim is extraordinarily realistic.

3 Red Skorba Figurines

The earliest representations of the human figure in Malta were a group of small female figurines found at Skorba.

4 Giant Goddess of Tarxien

Perhaps the most striking "Fat Lady", only the lower half of this giant statue survives. A replica is on site at Tarxien.

5 Shaman's Bundle

An intriguing group of pale figurines – human and animal – found at the Xagħra Circle.

6 Snake Relief

A huge stone found at Ġgantija is etched with an undulating snake. Its significance is still a mystery.

7 Bird Pot Sherd

This delicate potsherd from Ġgantija has a repeating pattern of a crested bird.

8 Animal Friezes

Sheep and pigs, all handsomely carved in relief, strut across a pair of stone apses discovered at Tarxien.

9 Altar Block

This stone altar from Tarxien, with spiral decoration, has a secret compartment where a flint knife and animal bones were found.

10 "The Priest"

This small figurine with a long skirt and a solemn face was found at Tarxien.

The best places to see Malta's archeological finds are the Museums of Archaeology in Valletta and Gozo **See pp40–41**

Left **Armoury, Grand Master's Palace** Right **Memorial to Jean de Lascaris in St John's Co-Cathedral**

🔟 Grand Masters

1 Philippe Villier de L'Isle Adam (1521–34)

L'Isle Adam was Grand Master when, in 1522, the Turks defeated the Order of St John and ousted it from Rhodes. The Knights looked for a permanent home for eight years until Charles V of Spain offered them the Maltese islands.

2 Jean Parisot de la Vallette (1557–68)

Brave and charismatic, La Vallette led the Knights in the Great Siege of 1565; he was 70 years old. He responded to Turkish attacks by firing back the heads of Turkish prisoners. After the victory, he began to build the city that bears his name.

3 Jean l'Evêque de la Cassière (1572–81)

La Cassière commissioned the building of St John's in Valletta as the conventual church of the Order. (It was granted Co-Cathedral status only in 1816.)

Jean l'Evêque de la Cassière

4 Alof de Wignacourt (1601–22)

Wignacourt's term of office was notable for the construction of several coastal fortifications, including the St Lucian Tower at Marsaxlokk and the Wignacourt Tower in St Paul's Bay. He also provided much of the funding for a new aqueduct to bring water from Ir-Rabat to Valletta *(see p88)*.

5 Jean de Lascaris Castellar (1636–57)

The Maltese still use the phrase *wiċċ Laskri* (face of Lascaris) for a sour facial expression, after this famously dour man. Like Wignacourt, he commissioned watchtowers and fortifications around the island, such as the Red Tower on Marfa Ridge *(see p80)*.

6 Nicolas Cotoner (1663–80)

Nicolas Cotoner followed his brother Raphael (Grand Master 1660–63). Together, these two Spanish Knights were responsible for the lavish decoration of the interior of St John's Co-Cathedral. Nicolas also strengthened the city walls, and ordered the construction of the Cottonera Lines and Fort Ricasoli, both of which protect the Three Cities *(see pp68–71)*.

7 Antoine Manoel de Vilhena (1722–36)

The Knights generally had as little as possible to do with the locals, but this Portuguese Grand Master was an exception; he did all he could to improve the lives of the Maltese population, and as a result achieved great popularity. He was also responsible for building the suburb of Floriana (just outside Valletta), the exquisite Manoel Theatre, and Fort Manoel in Marsamxett Harbour.

For more on St John's Co-Cathedral See pp10–13

8 Manoel Pinto de Fonseca (1741–73)

This vain, flamboyant and shrewd Grand Master gathered a huge court, which vied with the most fashionable in Europe. Under his rule, many of Valletta's restrained Renaissance buildings were embellished, including the Palace of the Grand Masters and the Auberge de Castille. He died at the age of 92; rumour has it that he owed his longevity to the elixirs concocted by his private alchemist.

Manoel Pinto de Fonseca

9 Ferdinand von Hompesch (1797–9)

Von Hompesch was a well-meaning Grand Master, but unsuited to a stand off with a cunning leader such as Napoleon. He oversaw the ignominious cession of Malta to the French, without a single shot being fired. (When Napoleon was defeated at Waterloo, Malta became British.)

10 Matthew Festing OBE (2008–)

The current – 79th – Grand Master is the order's second British head. He is primarily responsible for overseeing the Order's charitable activities.

Top 10 Unusual Facts about the Knights

1 Dining off Silver
Invalids in the Knights' Hospital dined off silver plate, for ease of cleaning.

2 Flamboyant Pinto
Among Pinto's staff was a baker whose only job was to make bread for the hounds.

3 English Knight
Sir Oliver Starkey, English secretary to La Vallette, is the only Knight below Grand Master buried in the crypt of St John's.

4 The Maltese Falcon
The Knights paid an annual tribute of a live falcon to the King of Spain – the historical nugget that inspired Dashiell Hammett's celebrated story.

5 Dragut Rais and La Vallette
These heroes on opposing sides during the Great Siege of 1565 had both previously spent time as galley slaves.

6 The Oubliette
Wrongdoers were confined in this dark hole in the rocks beneath Fort St Angelo.

7 Sex and Croquet
To keep his young Knights free of impurity, Grand Master Lascaris made them play *palla a maglio*, a version of croquet.

8 Valletta, Party Capital
By the 18th century, piety forgotten, Valletta was famous for promiscuity and hedonism.

9 Important Relics
When the Knights left Malta in 1798 *(see p13)*, they took the hand of St John the Baptist and other important relics with them.

10 Sovereign Knights of the Order of Malta
The Knights no longer have a permanent home, but claim sovereign (state-like) status.

The Grand Masters are the supreme leaders of the Order of the Knights of St John (see p13).

Left **St Paul's Cathedral, L-Imdina** Right **Our Lady's Return from Egypt, Comino**

Churches and Cathedrals

St John's Co-Cathedral, Valletta

St John's Co-Cathedral

One of Valletta's most iconic sights was built as the Knights' conventual church *(see pp10–13)*.

St Paul's Shipwreck Church, Valletta

For many, St Paul's arrival on the islands in AD 60 is the greatest event in Maltese history. In the depths of this Baroque church is a fragment of the pillar on which St Paul was beheaded and a venerated relic of the saint's wristbone.
⊗ *Triq San Pawl • Map J2 • 2122 3348 • Open 6:30am–12:30pm, 3–6:30pm Mon–Sat; 7am–noon, 4–6pm Sun • Free*

Church of St Lawrence, Il-Birgu

Knights and Maltese celebrated the end of the Great Siege here in 1565. Lorenzo Gafa designed the present church in 1681. It was restored after being damaged in World War II. ⊗ *Triq San Lawrenz • Map L5 • 2182 7057 • Open 9:30am–noon (till 10:30am Sun), 4:30–5:30pm daily • Free*

Our Lady of Victories Church, L-Isla

The original 18th-century church was destroyed in World War II but has been faithfully restored. The church contains statues of Our Lady of Victories, and of Christ the Redeemer, believed to have healing powers. ⊗ *Misrah Il-Papa Benedittu XV • Map K6 • 2182 7203 • Open daily for Mass from 7am • Free*

St Paul's Cathedral, L-Imdina

L-Imdina's cathedral is said to stand on the site of the villa of Roman Governor Publius, converted to Christianity by St Paul. Lorenzo Gafa designed today's elegantly restrained Baroque structure after an earthquake destroyed the original. ⊗ *Pjazza San Pawl • Map C4 • 2145 4136 • Open 9:30–4:45pm Mon–Sat, 3–4:30pm Sun • Free*

Mosta Dome, Il-Mosta

Officially Our Lady of the Assumption, this was built from 1833 to 1871. The dome is the third largest in Europe (or perhaps fourth; *see Xewkija Church, p39*). ⊗ *Pjazza Rotunda • Map C4 • 2143 3826 • Open 9–11:45am, 3–4:30pm Mon–Sat • Free*

Mosta Dome

Catholicism is the state religion in Malta, and 96 per cent of the population are practising Catholics.

Ta' Pinu Basilica, Gozo

Thousands of Maltese travel here hoping that Our Lady of Ta' Pinu will cure their ailments. Ex-voto offerings, from crutches to plaster casts, show the strength of their belief. ◈ *Near L-Gharb on the Ghammar road • Map D1 • 2155 6187 • Open 6:45am–7pm Mon–Sat; 6am–12:15pm, 1:30–7pm Sun) • Free*

Xewkija Church, Gozo

Xewkija Rotunda, completed in 1971, is claimed by Gozitans to have the third-largest dome in Europe – but this is disputed by the people of Il-Mosta *(see p38)*. The church can hold three times Ix-Xewkija's population. ◈ *St John the Baptist Square • Map E2 • 2155 6793 • Open daily for Mass • Free*

Gozo Cathedral nave, Ir-Rabat

Gozo Cathedral, Ir-Rabat/Victoria

Lorenzo Gafa designed this elegant Baroque cathedral, with its wonderful *trompe l'oeil* dome. ◈ *The Citadel • Map D2 • 2155 4101 • Open 5am–8pm daily • Free*

Our Lady's Return from Egypt, Comino

Set back from Santa Marija Bay, this winsome little church dates from the 13th century. The simple whitewashed building is topped with three hooped bells and surrounded by a grove of tamarisk trees. Mass is said twice a week. ◈ *Santa Marija Bay • Map A1 • 2155 6826 • Usually open Sat eve and Sun morning; check in advance • Free*

Top 10 Religious Figures

1 St Paul
In AD 60, St Paul was shipwrecked off the islands; he converted the local populace to Christianity.

2 St Agatha
A patron saint of Malta, St Agatha is said to have hidden from her Roman persecutors in a cave in Ir-Rabat.

3 St Publius
Roman Governor Publius was converted to Christianity by St Paul and was appointed first Bishop of Malta.

4 St John the Baptist
St John has been patron saint of the Knights since the Order was founded.

5 Pope Pius V
Pius V helped to pay for the construction of Valletta and sent his best engineers to advise on the project.

6 Our Lady of the Assumption
The most popular incarnation of the Virgin Mary in Malta. Her feast day, on 15 August, is one of the liveliest *festas*.

7 Our Lady of Ta' Pinu
Our Lady of Ta' Pinu is credited with miraculous healing powers *(see left)*.

8 Saint Peter
The feast day of Saints Peter and Paul on 29 June has fused with the traditional Maltese festival of L-Imnarja.

9 San Lawrenz
Unique as the only patron saint to have a Maltese village named after him, in Gozo.

10 St Andrew
Patron saint of fishermen, St Andrew's statue appears in lamp-lit niches across the islands. There's also a statue on the seafront in Ix-Xlendi.

Left **National Museum of Fine Arts** Right **Lascaris War Rooms, Valletta**

Museums and Arts Centres

1 National Museum of Archaeology, Valletta

A visit is essential to understand fully Malta's unique early history. Star attractions are the enigmatic "Sleeping Lady" (about 2000 BC), the Horus and Anubis pendant and a ceramic anthropomorphic sarcophagus from the Phoenician period. ✆ *Triq Ir-Repubblika • Map H2 • 2122 1623 • Open daily 8am–7pm •Adm charge • www.heritagemalta.org*

2 National Museum of Fine Arts, Valletta

Highlights include works by Mattia Preti (1613–99) and a watercolour of Valletta by the British artist J.M.W. Turner (1775–1851), who never set foot in the islands. There are also delicate sculptures by Antonio Sciortino (1879–1947). ✆ *Admiralty House, Triq Nofs In-Nahar • Map H2 • 2122 5769 • Open 9am–4:30pm daily • Adm charge*

"Sleeping Lady" – National Museum of Archaeology

3 Museum of St John's Co-Cathedral, Valletta

On display are treasures of the Knights, including vestments, portraits of Grand Masters (look out for Antoine de Favray's rendition of the decadent Pinto), tapestries and the monstrance built to hold the reliquary of the right hand of St John the Baptist. ✆ *Misrah San Ġwann • Map J2 • 2122 0536 • Open 9:30am–4:30pm Mon–Fri; 9:30am–noon Sat • Adm charge*

4 St James Cavalier Centre for Creativity, Valletta

This contemporary arts centre opened in 2000 for the millennium, and is now one of Malta's most dynamic and popular institutions. The emphasis is on events: theatre and film performances, concerts, children's events, workshops, even yoga classes. ✆ *Misrah Kastilja • Map H3 • 2122 3200 • Open 10am–9pm daily • Free • www.sjcav.org*

5 Lascaris War Rooms, Valletta

This fascinating museum is located in military operation rooms deep in the bastions of Valletta, which were used by the British as a secret headquarters during World War II and by NATO during the Cold War in the 1960s to monitor Soviet submarines. ✆ *Lascaris Ditch • Map H3 • 2123 4717 • Open 10am–5pm daily • Adm charge*

6 Fortifications Interpretation Centre, Valletta

Games, 3-D puzzles and a multilingual guide are part of the exhibition held in this magnificent building, apt for visits with the family. ✆ *St Mark Street • Map H2 • 2122 8594 • Open Jun–Sep: 9am–1pm Mon, Wed, Fri, Sat, 9am–4pm Tue, Thu; Oct–May: 10am–4pm Mon, Wed, Fri, 10am–7pm Tue, Thu, 9:30am–1pm Sat–Sat • Free*

Exhibits in Maltese museums are not always well labelled, but curators are generally happy to give explanations to visitors.

7 Malta Maritime Museum, Il-Birgu

Exhibits here range from model ships to lavish ceremonial barges built for the Grand Masters. Look out for the traditional decorations from fishing boats, including a wonderful St George and the dragon. ⊗ *Xatt Ir-Risq • Map K5 • 2166 0052 • Open daily 9am–4:30pm • Adm charge • www.heritagemalta.org*

Malta Maritime Museum

8 Cathedral Museum, L-Imdina

The collection here ranges from worn Roman tombstones to a fine 16th-century *Hagiothecium* (Book of Saints) and works by the German artist Albrecht Dürer (1471–1528). ⊗ *Pjazza L'Arċisqof • Map C4 • 2145 4697 • Open 9:30am–4:45pm Mon–Sat, 3–4:30pm Sun • Adm charge*

9 Museum of Archaeology, Ir-Rabat/Victoria, Gozo

This delightful museum is set in a noble mansion. Ancient Gozitan artifacts are displayed. ⊗ *Triq Bieb L'Imdina • Map D2 • 2155 6144 • Open daily 9am–5pm • Adm charge • www. heritagemalta.org*

10 Folklore Museum, Ir-Rabat/Victoria, Gozo

This engaging museum occupies three historic houses. Exhibits cover all aspects of rural life in Gozo, with recreations of traditional homes and a display of crafts and trades. ⊗ *Triq Bernardo DeOpuo • Map D2 • 2156 2034 • Open daily 9am–5pm • Adm charge • www.heritagemalta.org*

Top 10 Artists and Architects

1 Francesco Buonamici (1490–1562)
This celebrated Italian engineer designed Valletta's first major Baroque buildings.

2 Gerolamo Cassar (1520–92)
Cassar was responsible for the Grand Masters' Palace and St John's Co-Cathedral.

3 Francesco Laparelli da Cortona (1521–71)
The Pope sent Laparelli (once Michelangelo's assistant) to oversee the building of Valletta.

4 Matteo Perez d'Aleccio (1547–1616)
This pupil of Michelangelo created the Great Siege frieze in the Grand Masters' Palace.

5 Tommaso Dingli (1591–66)
Dingli designed Malta's most beautiful Renaissance churches, including St Mary's in H'Attard.

6 Mattia Preti (1613–99)
Painter of the nave in St John's Co-Cathedral, Preti was perhaps Malta's finest artist.

7 Lorenzo Gafa (1638–1703)
An outstanding Baroque architect, Gafa designed L-Imdina and Gozo cathedrals.

8 Andrea Belli (1703–22)
Belli remodelled the Auberge de Castille for Grand Master Pinto, adding superb Baroque flourishes.

9 Antoine de Favray (1706–91)
See this French-born artist's portraits and landscapes at the National Museum of Fine Arts.

10 J.M.W. Turner (1775–1851)
Turner painted his renowned watercolour of the Grand Harbour from a postcard.

Left **Blue Lagoon, Comino** Right **Dingli Cliffs**

🔟 Areas of Natural Beauty

1 Dwejra, Gozo
Spectacular cliffs, rocks with supposedly magical powers and curving bays make this stretch of Gozitan coastline among the most scenic regions in the entire Maltese islands (see pp26–7).

2 San Blas Bay, Gozo
This secluded beach can be found at the end of a lush valley filled with fruit trees, and its reddish sand makes a striking contrast with the green of the orchards. There is no direct road for access and just one kiosk in summer, so it is almost always wonderfully peaceful. ◉ Map F1
• Signposted from In-Nadur

3 Ta' Ċenċ Cliffs, Gozo
These sheer, silvery cliffs are hauntingly lovely, particularly at dusk. Wonderful walking trails follow the line of the cliff edge, and the pock-marked limestone landscape is etched with the mysterious Bronze Age "cart ruts".

Ta' Ċenċ Cliffs, Gozo

Dwejra, Gozo

Although illegal hunting remains a problem in the area, these cliffs are home to protected sea and coastal birds, including the blue rock thrush. ◉ Map E2

4 Salt Pans, Gozo
The salt pans are formed by shallow indentations in the creamy limestone, right on the water's edge. In winter storms, the pans fill with sea water, which evaporates in the summer heat to leave behind chunky white crystals of salt. The pools, glassy in winter and oddly pale in summer, have a peculiar yet haunting beauty. ◉ Map D1
• Between Xwieni Bay and Reqqa Point

5 Blue Lagoon, Comino
The beautiful Blue Lagoon is formed by a narrow channel which cuts between the small island of Comino and minute Cominetto. The azure waters are shallow and inviting, perfect for swimming, snorkelling and diving. Go out of season if you can, because the Lagoon's languid charms are shattered in summer by the crowds and the motor boats (see p28).

6 Marfa Ridge

This is the wildest and least populated part of the island of Malta. It was historically impossible to defend, which is why few settlements grew up here. The coast is pocked with little bays and beaches (the best are Paradise Bay and Little Armier), and the towering cliffs of Ras Il-Qammieħ rear up at the southwestern end. ⊛ *Map B2*

7 Fomm Ir-Riħ Bay

This wild and remote bay is surrounded by gentle hills with tumbling terraces of pale stone. The only way to get down to the bay is via a steep stone staircase hacked into the rock. As a result it has one of the few beaches in Malta to remain relatively uncrowded in summer. ⊛ *Map A4*

8 Dingli Cliffs

A thrilling road skirts these cliffs, 300 m (1,000 ft) high, which plunge dramatically into the inky sea. This is easily the loveliest and least spoilt corner of Malta, and is particularly beautiful during spring and autumn when the fields are carpeted with wild flowers. Take a picnic of fresh Maltese bread, some pungent local cheese and tomatoes with you. ⊛ *Map B5*

9 Buskett Gardens

In a fairly barren island, the Buskett Gardens stand out as Malta's most extensive woodlands. They were first established as a hunting ground for the Knights, and are filled with groves of olives, citrus trees and plump, bushy pines that look like gigantic broccoli.

Buskett Gardens

Perfect for picnics and leafy walks, these woods are the scene of one of Malta's most enjoyable festivals, L-Imnarja (see p48). ⊛ *Map C5*

10 Blue Grotto, Wied Iż-Żurrieq

This huge natural arch in the cliffs near the tiny village of Wied Iż-Żurrieq gets its name from the unearthly blue which seems to flicker beneath the waters, evoking thoughts of the mermaids who were believed to live here. A boat trip takes in this and six other caves along the same stretch of coast. ⊛ *Map D6 • Boats depart from Wied Iż-Żurrieq about every 15 mins, 9am–5pm (7pm in high season) daily*

Malta's infamous ex-prime minister Dom Mintoff used to ride his horse down the slippery steps of Fomm Ir-Riħ Bay.

43

Left **Marfa Ridge** Right **Salt pans near Wied Il-Għasri**

Walks and Drives

1 Floriana (walk)

Floriana is a town of faded Baroque beauty right at the gates of Valletta. Begin a short tour (1.5 km; 1 mile) by strolling along the Mall, then continue to the Sarria Chapel, decorated by Mattia Preti. Wander through the adjacent Botanic Gardens before visiting the Lion Fountain and turning back towards Valletta. ◈ *Map G3, H3*

2 Circuit of Comino (walk)

This 8-km (5-mile) walk takes a couple of hours. Begin at the Blue Lagoon and take the dirt road to Santa Marija Bay. Follow the curve of the headland (no marked path) to the highest point of Comino. Walk towards St Mary's Battery, then continue around the coast to the Comino Tower and back to the Blue Lagoon. ◈ *Map A1*

3 Victoria Lines: Fomm Ir-Riħ to Baħar iċ-Ċagħaq (walk)

This long, 30-km (19-mile) coast-to-coast hike follows the remnants of the Victoria Lines, British-built fortified walls. Begin at wild Fomm Ir-Riħ (or at L-Imġarr if relying on public transport), and follow the walls through cliffs and valleys to Baħar iċ-Ċagħaq. ◈ *Map A4*

4 Wied Il-Għasri and Salt Pans, Gozo (walk)

This is a circular 12-km (7-mile) route from Ir-Rabat/Victoria. Head for L-Għasri, then follow the signs for the Wied Il-Għasri, a blaze of colour in spring. Follow the coastline towards Marsalforn to see the salt pans scooped from limestone, and from Marsalforn walk back to Victoria. ◈ *Map D2*

5 Is-Siġġiewi to Ħad-Dingli (walk)

This walk (10 km; 6 miles) takes in the stunning Dingli Cliffs. Begin in Is-Siġġiewi, pass the chapel of Tal-Providenza, and reach the cliffs at the Underground Chapel. Follow the cliffs to the giant golf-ball of Ħad-Dingli radar station. Continue on to Ħad-Dingli to pick up the bus back. ◈ *Map C5*

6 Delimara Point (walk)

A circular 8-km (5-mile) walk from Marsaxlokk takes in both sides of the point. Make for the bay of Il-Ħofra Żgħira, follow the coast to Peter's Pool for a dip, then to Delimara Point. Return the other side for views of Marsaxlokk Bay. ◈ *Map F6*

Victoria Lines

Comino

7 Ix-Xlendi to San Lawrenz, Gozo (walk)

This arduous 12-km (7-mile) walk includes the stunning Dwejra Cliffs. From Xlendi Bay, climb up Tar-Riefnu then continue to Wardija Point. Follow the track to Dwejra Bay, then the path behind the chapel to San Lawrenz. ◈ Map D2

8 Marfa Ridge (walk)

A 14-km (9-mile) circuit from Mellieħa Bay takes in all of rugged Marfa Ridge. Head for the Ras il-Qammieħ cliffs, then follow the coast to Ċirkewwa and Aħrax Point, before heading back around the coast to Mellieħa Bay. ◈ Map A2

9 North Coast, Gozo (drive)

From Ir-Rabat/Victoria, head for pretty L-Għarb and Ta' Pinu Basilica, then Iz-Żebbuġ. Lunch in Marsalforn, then drive east to Calypso's cave and Ramla Bay to swim, then return via Ix-Xagħra to Ir-Rabat/Victoria. ◈ Map D1

10 West Coast, Malta (drive)

From Il-Qrendi, head for the Ħaġar Qim and Mnajdra temples. Drive on narrow roads to Laferla Cross, then follow signs for the "Clapham Junction" cart ruts and a breathtaking cliff view. Take the cliff road to Ħad-Dingli. ◈ Map D6

Top 10 Viewpoints

1 Upper Barrakka Gardens, Valletta
The beautiful gardens, with their fountains and flowers, frame magnificent views over the stunning Grand Harbour.

2 Dingli Cliffs Viewpoint
At the half-way point on the cliff road along Dingli Cliffs is a spectacular viewpoint. Park and walk to the headland.

3 Red Tower, Marfa Ridge
This squat, crenellated tower high on the ridge offers views over much of Malta and across to Comino and Gozo.

4 Citadel Walls, Ir-Rabat/Victoria, Gozo
Climb to the very top of the ramparts for great views over Gozo's verdant central plain.

5 Xewkija Dome, Gozo
The lift in Ix-Xewkija's church takes you to the top of the huge dome for spectacular views over all of Gozo.

6 Qammieh Point, Marfa Ridge
From here the massive cliffs of the beautiful, wild coastline stretch in both directions.

7 Dwejra Point, Gozo
Gozo's western coast, with its mighty cliffs and spectacular natural rock formations, looks beautiful from this high point.

8 L-Imdina's Ramparts
From here you can see major landmarks, including the enormous Mosta Dome.

9 Senglea Tower
This curious tower, in tiny gardens on the tip of L-Isla, offers lovely views of Valletta across the Grand Harbour.

10 Wignacourt Tower, St Paul's Bay
This lookout tower, built by the Knights, affords far-reaching views out over the bay.

➲ For more on the "Clapham Common" cart ruts See p35

Left **Ramla Bay, Gozo** Right **St Peter's Pool**

Beaches and Resorts

1 St Peter's Pool, Marsaxlokk

This perfect bay of turquoise water is surrounded by limestone cliffs as pale and creamy as Italian ice cream. The sea is clear and inviting – but watch out for occasional shoals of jellyfish. The pool is a rewarding end to a walk along the Delimara Peninsula, or it can also be reached by fishing boat from Marsaxlokk. ✆ *Map F6*

2 Tas-Sliema and St Julian's

These are the two major towns within the urban sprawl that stretches northwest of Valletta. The majority of Malta's hotels, restaurants, bars and clubs are concentrated in this area, making it the most popular tourist resort in the Maltese islands. Although there are no sandy beaches, several lidos are dotted along the rocky coast. ✆ *Map D4, E4*

Tas-Sliema and St Julian's

St Paul's Bay

3 St Paul's Bay

St Paul's Bay is the most attractive of the clutch of resorts that line the shores of the large bay of the same name. Its minuscule port, with its fleet of brightly painted *luzzus*, is still utterly charming. A church is built on the site where St Paul is said to have come ashore after his shipwreck in AD 60. ✆ *Map C3*

4 Mellieħa Bay

The sizeable resort town of Il-Mellieħa sits high on a ridge overlooking the sea. At the bottom of the hill is the sweep of golden sand that has made this resort one of the most popular with families. The sand, shallow waters and excellent amenities are perfect for parents with young children. ✆ *Map B2*

5 Għajn Tuffieħa Bay and Golden Bay

Two of Malta's most beautiful beaches, these are separated by a wonderful, though challenging, walking path. Golden Bay *(see p82)* is the more accessible and therefore not quite as charming as its little sister. ✆ *Map B2*

Ramla Bay, Gozo

Gozo's prettiest beach, with ochre sands and crystal-clear waters, Ramla Bay is best in the "shoulder" seasons (May–Jun and Sep–Oct), before the crowds arrive or after they have left, yet it's warm enough to swim and picnic. There are a couple of beach cafés and you can strike out along coastal paths in both directions. It is overlooked by Calypso's Cave (see p100), at the end of a short but stiff uphill walk that is rewarded by magnificent views. Map E1

Marsalforn, Gozo

Marsalforn is Gozo's largest resort, yet this former fishing village remains enjoyably low-key, and is ideal for a quiet and relaxing holiday. Piled along a ridge on the northern coast, it has all the amenities you would expect, including restaurants, bars and water-sports facilities. There's some fine walking along this stretch of coast. Take a stroll to the salt pans (see p42); carved into the limestone, they glimmer beautifully in the sun. Map E1

Ix-Xlendi, Gozo

Ix-Xlendi enjoys a dramatic setting, strung out between powerful cliffs and overlooking an attractive bay. Thoughtless development has almost entirely destroyed the village itself, but the scenic backdrop is still more or less intact. Sleepy by the standards of most resorts, this is Gozo's liveliest holiday town and has all the amenities you would expect. Map D2

Blue Lagoon, Comino

The dazzling turquoise waters and remote island setting make this the most celebrated beauty spot in all Malta. Although there is no beach as such, the flat rocks around the lagoon fill up in summer with sun-worshippers and families enjoying the shallow, child-friendly waters. The Blue Lagoon is also a great spot for diving and snorkelling, but it's quietest early or late (see p28).

Santa Marija Bay, Comino

Santa Marija Bay, Comino

This lovely bay with its sandy beach is overlooked by a charming little pink-painted police station (with a flag to show when the local officer is making his weekly visit). The rugged headland has rocky coves and fine cliff walks. It's very popular in summer, but empties when the day-trippers leave (see p29).

Malta boasts some of the clearest waters in the Mediterranean – just one of the reasons why it's a favourite diving destination.

Left **Carnival** Right **Good Friday celebrations in Il-Mosta**

Festivals and Other Events

Carnival
1 The Knights brought Carnival to Malta in the 16th century. It takes place in the week leading up to Ash Wednesday, and has always been an excuse to let off steam before Lent begins. It is celebrated in villages across the islands with parades, fireworks and fancy dress. The biggest events are in Valletta and Floriana; In-Nadur, on Gozo, is infamous for its own rather unruly version.

Good Friday
2 Malta is staunchly Catholic, and Good Friday is marked with suitable solemnity. Statues of scenes from the Passion of Christ are paraded through the streets of towns all over the islands.

Easter Sunday
3 In contrast to sombre Good Friday, Easter Sunday is a much more joyful affair. There are more parades, but they include music

Fireworks Festival, Grand Harbour, Valletta

and sometimes even fireworks. *Figolli* (pastry figures filled with marzipan) are exchanged, along with chocolate eggs and rabbits.

Fireworks Festival
4 The Maltese love fireworks, and every year they show off their prowess using the spectacular Grand Harbour as the theatre. Other countries are invited to participate, and for three consecutive nights the Grand Harbour is ablaze with colour and sound. It's not to be missed if you are in the islands. ✪ *Apr/May*

L-Imnarja
5 One of Malta's most colourful events, this traditional folklore festival is celebrated with music, dance, song and local foods such as *fenkata* ("rabbit feast"). The main arena is Buskett Gardens, where there are bareback horse and donkey races, as well as the traditional singing known as *Għana*. The carousing carries on all night. ✪ *28/29 Jun*

Local Festas
6 Every village in Malta and Gozo joyfully celebrates the feast day of its patron saint with gaudy lighting and street decorations, brass bands, parades, firework shows, traditional foods and plenty of local wine. The flamboyant parish churches are trimmed with coloured lights, and each village competes to put on the best and wildest *festa*. ✪ *Throughout summer*

Ash Wednesday falls on 18 Feb in 2015 and 10 Feb in 2016; Carnival takes place during the previous week.

7 Jazz Festival

Major international performers are invited to the fabulous three-day jazz festival that is held on Barriera Wharf, Valletta, in the Grand Harbour. The setting is magical, and a variety of musical styles is represented. ◈ *Jul*
• www.maltajazzfestival.com

8 Malta International Air Show

A great family event, Malta's annual air show displays modern and vintage aircraft which can be explored, plus flying displays. You can see historic aircraft such as Spitfires and Hurricanes in action and enjoy the aerial dexterity of international aerobatic teams.
◈ *Sep* • www.maltairshow.com

Isle of MTV, Malta Music Week

9 Isle of MTV

A highlight of the Malta Music Week, this event has been graced by the likes of Enrique Iglesias, Jessie J and Lady Gaga in the past. Young-sters and music lovers throng to Floriana, outside Valletta, to watch live performances by top artists. ◈ *Jun* • www.isleofmtv.com

10 Christmas Celebrations

A country with a population that is mainly Catholic, Malta celebrates Christmas with gusto. Beautiful lights adorn the city of Valletta and in some years, a village is turned into a live crib for a re-enactment of the nativity scene. ◈ *Dec*

Top 10 Festival Traditions

1 Brass Bands
The British introduced this tradition, which has been enthusiastically embraced.

2 Traditional Foods
Local nougat (*qubbajt*) is eaten at all festivals. During L-Imnarja, it's traditional to eat rabbit (*fenek*), and at Easter, marzipan-stuffed pastry *figolli*.

3 Pilgrimages
The devout Maltese make pilgrimages to holy sites such as St Paul's Grotto in Ir-Rabat or the Ta' Pinu Basilica in Gozo.

4 Penitents
Penitents follow the floats of Easter processions dressed in pointed hoods. Many are barefoot or carry heavy crosses.

5 Folk Dances
Folk dances are performed in traditional dress. Among them are *il-Maltija* and the *parata*, performed with sticks.

6 Floats
The Maltese take decorations for festivals very seriously. Carnival floats are particularly flamboyant.

7 Confetti
On village feast days, children toss confetti from balconies as the main statue from the church is paraded.

8 Street Decorations
Maltese street decorations are dazzling – literally. Lines of light bulbs outline the church and often the houses too.

9 Fireworks
Fireworks are the soul of every village *festa*; Ħal Lija and L-Imqabba are famous for them.

10 Petards
For weeks leading up to the local summer *festas*, chil-dren tear around their villages letting off these fire crackers.

Left **Preparing to dive at the Blue Hole, Dwejra, Gozo** Right **Golf at the Royal Malta Golf Club**

⑩ Outdoor Activities

1 Diving and Snorkelling

Maltese waters are renowned for diving and snorkelling. Natural harbours, bays, wrecks, reefs and caves offer endless opportunities for experienced and novice divers alike. The water is warm and clear, and there is a wealth of marine life. Contact the Professional Diving Schools Association for information on dives and schools. ✎ *Msida Court, 61 Msida Sea Front • Map E4 • info@pdsa.org.mt • www.pdsa.org.mt*

Ghadira Wetland Reserve bird sanctuary

2 Sailing

Malta has a maritime tradition dating back thousands of years, and yachting is very popular. The biggest marinas are to be found in Marsamxett Harbour *(see p106)*.

3 Other Water Sports

Most hotels can arrange jet-skis, water-skiing, para-sailing, windsurfing and so on. The best windsurfing areas are Il-Mellieħa and Baħar iċ-Ċagħaq. Water polo is a popular spectator sport – in fact, it's a national obsession.

Windsurfing

4 Hiking

Both Malta and Gozo boast excellent hiking trails *(see pp44–5)*; Gozo has the edge because it is much less crowded. Comino is also great for a hike (albeit a short one), if only because few visitors venture beyond the bays. Watch out for Maltese hunters *(see p111)*.

5 Bird-watching

Hunters and trappers have done their best to wipe out the Maltese bird population, but they haven't succeeded yet. They eliminated the Mediterranean peregrine falcon from the beautiful Ta' Ċenċ cliffs, but this area is still home to all kinds of birdlife, including the largest colony of breeding Cory's Shearwaters in the Maltese islands. There are two bird sanctuaries in Malta *(see p79)*.

6 Golf

Malta has just one golf course, the Royal Malta Golf Club. It is open to visitors daily except Thursday and Saturday mornings, but advance booking is essential. Facilities include changing rooms, bar, restaurant, pro shop, practice putting green and driving range. Equipment can be hired, and lessons are available for golfers of all abilities. Note that "proper golf attire" (polo shirt, tailored trousers or shorts) is compulsory. ✎ *Triq Aldo Moro, Il-Marsa • Map D4 • 2122 3704 • www.royalmaltagolfclub.com*

Boat excursion, Crystal Lagoon, Comino

Boat Excursions

Numerous boat excursions are available, from a tour of the Grand Harbour to jaunts taking in all three main islands. In Malta, most trips start from Tas-Sliema, in Gozo from Xlendi Bay.

Rockclimbing

There are no mountains, but the cliffs offer exciting challenges for climbers. More than 1,200 established routes include climbs suitable for people of all abilities. The Malta Climbing Club can help plan your itinerary and offers advice on the best climbing spots. ❧ 9929 9836
• www.maltaclimbingclub.com

Horseriding

Malta has a long tradition of horseriding, and even boasts Europe's oldest polo club. There are numerous stables where you can arrange children's pony rides or longer treks for experienced riders. Malta's Tourism Authority can supply a list of approved centres. ❧ www.visitmalta.com

Cycling

The volume of traffic, terrible roads and appalling driving make cycling a bad idea on the island of Malta. On Gozo, the surfaces and drivers are just as bad, but the roads are generally very quiet. Be prepared for steep hills.

Top 10 Diving and Snorkelling Sites

1 Marfa Point, Ċirkewwa
Good for night dives, with moray eels, octopuses and corals. Has a training pool for beginners. ❧ Map A2

2 Ahrax Point
Off Marfa Ridge. Huge seaweed meadows shelter abundant marine life. Good visibility for photos. ❧ Map B2

3 Blenheim Bomber, Marsaxlokk
The remains of this World War II plane make for an interesting but difficult dive. ❧ Map F5

4 Delimara Point
This site is reached by boat. Groupers and stingrays are often seen. ❧ Map F6

5 Fungus Rock, Gozo
Several good sites cluster around Dwejra; this huge rock, covered in marine life, is one of the best. ❧ Map C1

6 Azure Window, Gozo
Another scenic dive at Dwejra. Huge boulders shelter abundant marine life. ❧ Map C1

7 The Blue Dome, or Cathedral Cave, Gozo
One of the best. Light reflects onto the vast ceiling, creating the "blue dome" effect. Fish include sea horses. ❧ Map D1

8 San Dimitri Point, Gozo
Accessible only by boat. There are shoals of barracuda and many other fish. ❧ Map C1

9 Lighthouse Reef, Comino
Perhaps Comino's best site, with a chimney through the reef. Marine life includes sea horses and starfish. ❧ Map A1

10 Santa Marija Caves, Comino
Several caves, some offering spectacular swim-throughs. A good photo spot. ❧ Map A1

Left **Malta Experience** Right **Mellieħa Bay**

Children's Activities

1 Malta Experience, Valletta
Malta has countless audio-visual attractions, mostly in Valletta and L-Imdina. This one offers a good introduction to Maltese history on a giant screen, but the 45-minute show may be a bit too long for smaller children.
◈ *Mediterranean Conference Centre, Triq Il-Mediterran • Map K2 • 2124 3776 • On the hour 11am–4pm Mon–Fri, 11am–2pm Sat, Sun (until 1pm Sun Jul–Sep) • Adm charge • www.themaltaexperience.com*

2 Underwater Safari
Take a trip on a glass-bottomed boat and see how many types of fish you can spot. The trip takes just over an hour and includes a fish-feeding session.
◈ *Buġibba, next to Bognor Beach • Map Q3 • Departs at 11am, 1pm & 3pm; Mon–Sat Jun–Sep, Mon–Fri Apr, May & Oct • Adm charge • www.captainmorgan.com.mt*

3 Mediterraneo Marine Park
This seaside marine park puts on daily shows by dolphins, sea lions and parrots. The reptile room and seal pool are also popular, but for many the highlight is the chance to swim with

Popeye Village

dolphins (book ahead, must be over 8 years). ◈ *Bahar Ic-Caghaq • Map D3 • 2137 2218 • Open daily 10am–5pm Mar–Oct (check for times rest of the year) • Adm charge • www.mediterraneo.com.mt*

4 Splash & Fun Water Park
It may not rival most European water parks but you will find a wave pool, a variety of slides and chutes and a play area for smaller kids here, plus plenty of organized fun and activities.
◈ *Bahar Ic-Caghaq • Map D3 • 2137 4283 • Open daily mid-May–early Oct (until 9pm late Jun–early Sep) • Adm charge • www.splashandfun.info*

5 Popeye Village, Anchor Bay
Popeye's home town of Sweethaven was recreated here for *Popeye, the Movie*. Besides the film set, younger children may also enjoy the adjoining fun park. ◈ *Map A3 • 2152 4782 • Open daily 9:30am–7pm • Adm charge • www.popeyemalta.com*

Mediterraneo Marine Park

As in most southern Mediterranean cultures, the Maltese adore children and will do everything they can to make yours welcome.

Playmobil Fun Park, Ħal-Far
Kids aged 6-plus can tour the world's second-largest Playmobil factory and see all their favourite characters being made. There's also a small play park, café and shop. Book the factory tour ahead. ⚅ *Ħal-Far Industrial Estate • Map E6 • 2224 2445 • Open daily 10am–6pm • www.playmobilmalta.com*

Malta Aviation Museum
Kids will enjoy seeing the large collection of vintage aircraft on display. The more technically minded can watch volunteers restoring the planes. ⚅ *Ta' Qali Aerodrome, between L-Imdina and Ħ'Attard • Map C4 • Open daily 9am–4pm • Adm charge • www.maltaaviationmuseum.com*

Malta National Aquarium
A walk-through tank and 130 different species of fish make this a wonderful place to visit with children. The outdoor play area is an added attraction. ⚅ *Triq it-Trunciera, San Pawl il-Baħar • Map C3 • 2258 8100 • Open daily 10am–10pm • Adm charge • www.aquarium.com.mt*

Eden SuperBowl
Ten-pin bowling can provide a welcome respite from soaring temperatures or rainy days. ⚅ *St George's Bay • Map D3 • 2371 0777 • Open daily, call to book • Adm charge*

Mellieħa Bay
This popular, sandy and shallow bay is good for families with small children *(see p46)*.

Malta National Aquarium

Top 10 Child-friendly Restaurants

The Avenue, Paċeville
A colourful, buzzy budget restaurant *(see p75)*.

Henry J. Beans American Bar & Grill, St Julian's
A 1950s-style burger-and-rib joint with an outdoor terrace. ⚅ *Corinthia San Ġorġ, St George's Bay • 2370 2694*

Piccolo Padre, St Julian's
A popular Italian restaurant serving great pasta and pizzas. ⚅ *194 Main Street • 2134 4875*

Hard Rock Café, St Julian's
The rock-themed decor features Cher's dress, and the menu the usual burgers and fajitas. ⚅ *Bay Street Hotel Complex, St George's Bay • 2372 2257*

Tal-Familja, Marsaskala
This friendly seafood spot is a favourite with Maltese families *(see p97)*.

Fontanella Tea Gardens, L-Imdina
Service may be slow, but kids seem to like these outdoor tea rooms *(see p89)*.

Blue Creek, Għar Lapsi
Overlooking the popular lido, this restaurant is very family-friendly *(see p97)*.

Tex Mex Grill & Cantina, Tas-Sliema
This raucous US-themed spot is always a hit with youngsters. ⚅ *89 Triq ix-Xatt • 2131 8943*

Gillieru, St Paul's Bay
A great family-friendly choice overlooking the bay *(see p83)*.

Mamma Mia
Delicious Mediterranean cuisine, a friendly ambience, and efficient service. ⚅ *Ta' Xbiex Seafront • 2133 7248*

Left **Bread vendor** Centre *Qubbajt* Right *Mqaret*

Culinary Highlights

1 Maltese Bread

The Maltese are justly proud of their excellent bread. Most villages have at least one bakery, where you can pick up delicious *hobz* (small soft rolls) or *ftira* (a ring-shaped loaf that is similar in texture to Italian *ciabatta*).

2 Gbejniet

These small round cheeselets are typical of Gozo and are made from goat or sheep's milk. There are two common kinds: the plain, which is smooth and creamy, and the peppered version, which is piquant and perfect with the local crusty bread and a slice of tomato. These cheeses are often used to flavour other dishes, such as soups.

3 Soppa Tal-armla

Maltese cuisine boasts many delicious soups, including *minestra* (vegetable soup) and the traditional *soppa tal-armla* (literally "widow's soup"). This

Ftira and gbejniet

TRADITIONAL SET MENU
Traditional Starters
LOCAL GOAT'S CHEESE SALAD.
VEGETABLE SOUP.
SPAGHETTI WITH RABBIT SAUCE.

Traditional Main Course
FRIED RABBIT IN GARLIC & WHITE WINE
GRILLED SWORDFISH
CHICKEN IN WHITE WINE & TOMATOES.

All main courses are served with vegetables & potatoes.

CHOICE OF COFFEE

Lm 3.75

Traditional menu including rabbit (fenek)

name probably comes from the simple ingredients, which include potatoes, courgettes and other vegetables, plus a dollop of ricotta cheese or a *gbejniet* cheeselet.

4 Bragioli

Bragioli are "beef olives", similar to the Italian version. They are made using slices of beef or veal stuffed with a mixture of cheese, ham and herbs, then braised gently on the stove or in the oven.

5 Fenek

Fenek (rabbit) is the most popular meat in Malta, and a favourite for *festas* and special events. It is prepared in countless ways, but the most common include rabbit stew made with wine and flavoured with herbs, rabbit fried with garlic and herbs, and a simple dish of spaghetti served with a rabbit sauce.

6 Torta Tal-lampuki

This fish pie is made with *lampuki*, a prized local fish that is only available for a short period each year (usually from September to November). Such is the demand for this fish that rights to catch it are granted by lottery. The pie combines the fish with vegetables, walnuts, olives and raisins, and is considered a great delicacy by locals.

Gbejniet *made with sheep's milk are considered superior in taste to those made with goats' or cows' milk.*

7 Qubbajt

This nougat-style sweet is made with almonds and honey, and is traditionally eaten at festivals and special events. There are always several stalls selling *qubbajt* at village *festas*, but it is also available year-round from stalls and local shops. It is said to date back to the Arab occupation of the islands.

8 Pastizzi and Qassatat

Pastizzi – Malta's favourite snack – are tasty, diamond-shaped pastry parcels stuffed with ricotta cheese or a pea mixture. *Pastizzi* stalls can be found everywhere, and virtually every old-fashioned bar will offer its own, home-made versions. *Qassatat* are similar to *pastizzi* but made of a lighter pastry and round in shape.

Qassatat

9 Hobz Biz-zejt

These are chunks of bread brushed with olive oil and topped with a mixture of roughly chopped tomatoes, onions and herbs. They were traditionally considered a humble snack, akin to Italian *crostini*, but have acquired a sophisticated cachet in recent years and are regularly served in smart bars and restaurants as appetizers.

10 Mqaret

Mqaret are scrumptious pastry parcels, filled with a date mixture and deep-fried. They make the perfect sweet snack, and are delicious, if fattening.

Top 10 Drinks

1 Ċisk Lager
An excellent lager beer, this is very refreshing on burning-hot summer days.

2 Hopleaf Pale Ale
A tasty amber ale that goes well with a couple of *pastizzi*. Like Ċisk, it's made by Farsons.

3 Blue Label Ale
This popular Farsons brew has a sweet, malty taste.

4 Wine
Maltese wine has improved a lot in recent years. The main producers are Marsovin, Delicata and Meridiana.

5 Kinnie
Peculiar to Malta, this is a slightly bitter, fizzy soft drink flavoured with orange and herbs.

6 Anisette
This aniseed-flavoured liqueur is a Gozitan speciality, and is an ingredient in many local pastries and biscuits.

7 Bajtra Liqueur
The fat, stumpy limbs of prickly pear cacti grow all over the islands. The red, ear-like fruits are used in this sweet liqueur, which is also flavoured with honey and herbs.

8 Coffee
Maltese coffee may sound Italian (*cappuccino, espresso*) but lacks the kick. It's served long and milky for breakfast.

9 Tea
The Maltese remain attached to tea, introduced by the British and often, especially in rural areas, very strong.

10 Bottled Water
Much of the tap water in Malta is produced by a "reverse osmosis" process (which converts sea water into drinking water). Most people prefer to drink bottled water, much of it produced locally.

Left **Giannini, Valletta** Right **Ta' Rikardu, Ir-Rabat/Victoria**

Restaurants

1 Giannini, Valletta
A town house with beautiful views over Marsamxett Harbour houses perhaps Valletta's best restaurant, with creative Maltese and Italian cuisine. The set menu "A journey through the Maltese Islands" is a good introduction to local cooking. ◈ 23 Triq L-Imitihen • Map H2 • 2123 7121 • Closed Sat L, Sun • €€€€€

2 Rubino, Valletta
One of the best places for traditional Maltese soups and stews. It began as a confectionery shop and is still famous for its desserts; the *cassata Siciliana* – a rich and creamy concoction made with ricotta cheese – is heavenly. ◈ 53 Triq Il-Fran • Map H2 • 2122 4656 • Closed Mon–Fri D, Tue–Sat L; reservations highly recommended • €€€

3 Da Pippo, Valletta
Frequented by celebrities, this welcoming, rustic-style trattoria is regularly voted as Valletta's best restaurant. All the food is fresh, homecooked and excellent value for money. Menu highlights are clam pasta and spaghetti with Maltese sausage. ◈ 136 Triq Melita • Map H2 • 2124 8029 • Open for lunch only; advance booking essential; closed Sun • €€€

4 Ta' Frenc, Marsalforn, Gozo
Housed in an exquisitely restored 14th-century farmhouse, the award-winning Ta' Frenc features Maltese and Mediterranean cuisine, with many ingredients from its own farm. Try Chef Mario's six-course menu or savour Gozo's fresh produce in the market menu dishes. ◈ Triq Għajn Damma (off Marsalforn Road) • Map E1 • 2155 3888 • Closed Tue • €€€€€

5 Jeffrey's, L-Għarb, Gozo
A friendly, simple restaurant in an old farmhouse, this has a lovely ivy-draped courtyard. Choose from traditional dishes such as fried Gozitan cheese, marrows stuffed with meat or fresh local fish. ◈ 10 Triq Gharb • Map D1 • 2156 1006 • Open Mon–Sat, advance booking essential; closed Jan • €

6 Ta' Rikardu, Ir-Rabat/ Victoria, Gozo
A great place for a simple meal of Gozitan cheese, tomatoes and fresh bread, washed down with a sturdy local wine. ◈ 4 Triq Il-Fosos • Map D2 • 2155 5953 • Closes 6pm (7pm in summer) • €€€

Rubino, Valletta

7 Waterbiscuit, St Julian's

This contemporary eatery serves delicious pumpkin gnocchi and local pork belly. It offers an interesting cocktail list and also has the option of alfresco dining. ◎ St George's Bay • Map N1 • 2736 2225 • €€

Grabiel, Marsaskala

8 Grabiel, Marsaskala

Grabiel is justly famous for its fresh and varied seafood. It also serves meat and pasta, but seafood is the star. ◎ Pjazza Mifsud Bonnici • Map F5 • 2163 4194 • Closed Sun D, Mon L • €€

9 La Dolce Vita, St Julian's

Enjoy delicious Italian food at this well-designed restaurant. The stylish interiors and splendid views of the sea enhance the experience of dining here. ◎ St George's Road • Map N1 • 7938 8660 • €€

10 Zeri's, St Julian's

Stylish and relaxed, this fashionable place overlooks the small harbour at Portomaso in St Julian's. The chef, Mark Zerafa ("Zeri"), prepares fresh, creative dishes, taking his inspiration from around the world. ◎ Portomaso Marina, St Julian's • Map N1 • 2135 9559 • €€€

Top 10 Food Shops

1 Smart Supermarket, Birkirkara
A good source of local meat, fresh fish, vegetables and Gozitan cheese. ◎ Triq In-Naxxar

2 Azzopardi's Fisheries, Tas-Sliema
This shop is highly praised for the variety and freshness of its seafood. ◎ Triq Tas-Sliema

3 Arkadia Foodstore, St Julian's
Sells the best of everything, with a butcher, fishmonger and grocer. ◎ Portomaso shopping complex, St Julian's

4 White Sheep, Il-Gzira
Delicacies such as French meats and Italian biscotti can be found at this store. ◎ Triq D'Argens, Il-Gzira

5 Ir-Razzett, Il-Mellieħa
Delicious fresh fruit and vegetables are the main attraction here. ◎ 244 Triq Ġorġ Borg Olivier

6 Busy Bee, Msida
A local favourite, especially for konnoli (fried pastry tubes stuffed with sweet ricotta). ◎ Ix-Xatt, Msida

7 Fish Market, Marsaxlokk
The busiest and most colourful fish market on the islands, held every Sunday.

8 Marsovin, Marsa
One of Malta's oldest winemakers; cellar tours (book ahead). ◎ www.marsovin.com

9 4 Triq Il Fosos, Ir-Rabat/Victoria, Gozo
This shop, next to Ta' Rikardu restaurant, sells traditional Gozitan thyme honey, anisette and local wines.

10 Delicata, Paola
Another leading wine-producer, also offering tours. ◎ Paola waterfront • 2182 5199

For a guide to restaurant price ranges See p67

AROUND MALTA & GOZO

MALTA'S TOP 10

Left **Grand Master's Palace** Right **Summer dining room, Casa Rocca Piccola**

Around Valletta

VALLETTA, A GLORIOUS CITY OF GOLDEN STONE, *straddles a narrow promontory flanked on either side by magnificent natural harbours. Built for the Knights after the Great Siege of 1565 and named after their victorious Grand Master, Jean Parisot de la Vallette, this fortress city is contained behind a massive ring of impenetrable walls and bastions. Within the walls, the Renaissance streets unfold in an elegant grid. Valletta's heart is broad Triq Ir-Repubblika, Republic Street, lined with princely palaces and dominated by the spectacular Co-Cathedral of St John. From here, side streets flanked by* crumbling palazzi slope steeply down to the harbours. Time, neglect and the terrible bombardment of World War II have all taken their toll on this miniature capital, and yet its cobbled streets remain hauntingly redolent of the era of the Knights. Still dreaming of the past, the somnolent city shuts down at nightfall.

Manoel Theatre

Preceding pages **A view of L-Imdina Cathedral from outside the city walls**

St John's Co-Cathedral

St John's Co-Cathedral
Although the magnificent Co-Cathedral may be severe and unembellished on the outside, inside it explodes in a glorious visual paean to the wealth and influence of the powerful Knights (see pp10–13).

Palace of the Grand Masters
This spectacular palace, filled with opulent tapestries and paintings, was the magnificent residence of the Grand Masters of the Order of the Knights of St John for more than two centuries (see pp8–9).

Auberges of the Langues
Each of the eight langues – literally "tongues", national branches of the Order of St John – had its own inn, or auberge, in newly built 16th-century Valletta. They were grand lodging houses for the Knights, and monuments to their wealth and prestige. Most of the few surviving auberges are now government offices and are not open to the public, but their graceful Baroque façades epitomize Valletta's regal allure. The most lavish is the Auberge de Castille et Leon (on Misrah

Kastilja), now the office of the Maltese president. The former Auberge de Provence houses the National Museum of Archaeology. Look out too for the Auberge d'Italie, on Triq Il-Merkanti, and the discreet Auberge d'Aragon, opposite St Paul's Anglican Cathedral. ◈ Map H3, H2, H3, J1

National Museum of Archaeology
The old Auberge de Provence, its former magnificence somewhat battered, is the setting for this collection of fascinating artifacts gathered from Malta's prehistoric temples. Two of the star attractions are the serene and lovely "Sleeping Lady" (see p40) and the "Venus of Malta."

National Museum of Fine Arts
A sweet but rather faded 16th-century palazzo with a fine Baroque staircase houses this delightful museum, which contains many paintings, sculptures and items of furniture by Maltese and overseas artists (see p40).

"Venus of Malta", National Museum of Archaeology

Auberge de Castille et Leon

➡ For more on artifacts discovered in Malta's prehistoric temples See p35

St James Cavalier Centre for Creativity

6 St James Cavalier Centre for Creativity

One of the mighty bastions that protect the main gate into the city has been sympathetically and beautifully restored. It now houses this excellent centre for contemporary arts, with a theatre, cinema and galleries *(see p40)*. There's also a delightful café, Inspirations, with an outdoor terrace in summer *(see p66)*.

7 Lascaris War Rooms

These dank, sunless rooms deep in Valletta's bastions were the nerve centre for military operations during World War II. Field Marshal Montgomery and General Eisenhower were among the Allied commanders based here. The wartime atmosphere is recreated with models and equipment *(see p40)*.

Malta and the Movies

Valletta's Grand Harbour is spectacularly cinematic, ringed by honey-coloured spires and bastions which have barely changed in centuries. The Maltese islands have provided the backdrop for countless films, including *Troy*, *Gladiator*, *Midnight Express*, *The League of Extraordinary Gentlemen*, *Swept Away* and *A Different Loyalty*.

8 Manoel Theatre

The Manoel is one of the oldest surviving enclosed theatres in Europe. It was built in 1731 by Grand Master Manoel de Vilhena. The auditorium is much smaller than in modern theatres, oval and lined with three tiers of boxes on which a delicate, gilded Mediterranean scene was painted. A particularly lavish box, reserved for the Grand Master, is now used by the Maltese president. A seat is still reserved for the censor, who retains enormous influence in this deeply Catholic country. The stage and orchestra pit are tiny, so large modern productions, such as ballets, can rarely be mounted. The adjoining theatre museum contains fascinating 19th-century machinery for making dramatic sound effects, including thunder and heavy winds. The café is one of the nicest in Valletta *(see p65)*. ◐ Triq It-Teatru L'Antik • Map J2 • 2559 5523 • Guided visits begin every 45 minutes, 9:30am–4pm Mon–Fri, 9:30am–noon Sat • Adm charge • www. teatrumanoel.com.mt

9 St Paul's Shipwreck Church

Dedicated to Malta's premier patron saint, this elaborate Baroque church was built between 1639 and 1740 on the site of an earlier, simpler church by Gerolamo Cassar *(see p41)*. The façade was added in 1885 by Nicola Zammit *(see p38)*.

10 Casa Rocca Piccola

This exquisite palace was built in the 16th century for an Italian Knight, but it has belonged to the noble de Piro family for the last two centuries. The 9th

Marquis de Piro has opened his family home to the public, and runs entertaining and witty guided tours around the 50-room palazzo. (The Marquis doesn't personally lead all the tours, so it's best to ensure in advance that he'll be your guide.) The rooms contain some beautiful items of furniture and fascinating curiosities, such as a pouch of silver medical instruments – among the very few silver objects to survive Napoleon's rapacious troops. There's also an ornate 18th-century sedan chair. The family portraits and photographs, and the quirky curio collections, lend the house a warm and personal ambience not usually found in stately homes. Underneath the palazzo, the old water cisterns were converted into a bomb shelter during World War II. They are connected by passages to the pretty patio with its pots of colourful flowers. ✆ 74 Triq Ir-Repubblika • Map J2 • 2122 1499 • Adm by guided visit only, on the hour 10am–4pm Mon–Sat • Adm charge • www. casaroccapiccola.com

St Paul's Shipwreck Church

A Day in Valletta

Morning

Take a bus to the Triton Fountain facing the city entrance. Stop at the **mqaret stall** for a date pastry before heading through the main gate. Sweep down Triq Ir-Repubblika to **St John's Co-Cathedral** (see pp10–13), the most splendid church in the Maltese islands. After visiting the cathedral, have a coffee out on the square at the **Caffe Cordina** (see p66). Continue down Triq Ir-Repubblika to the charming **Casa Rocca Piccola**, where the Marquis will give you a tour of his family home if you pre-book. Have a snack at one of the cafés on Merchant Street before stopping by the **Manoel Theatre** (see p65). Lunchtime concerts are often held here – check in advance with the tourist office.

Afternoon

Return to Triq Ir-Repubblika and make for the Auberge de Provence, now home to the fascinating **National Museum of Archaeology** (see p40). A visit will help you to put Malta's extraordinary temple culture into context. Don't miss the upstairs salon or the beautiful and mysterious megalithic sculpture of the Sleeping Lady. Stroll over to the **Upper Barrakka Gardens**, which are small but beautifully kept, for spellbinding views over the Grand Harbour. The view is best at dusk, extending across the water to the romantic silhouette of the Three Cities (see pp68–71). Take the elevator down to Valletta and walk along the waterfront to pick your preferred bar or restaurant.

Left **Triq Ir-Repubblika** Right **Agenda Bookshop**

Shopping

"Monti" Market
Crowds pack this street market every morning to buy fashion items, CDs, leather goods, souvenirs and more. There's a bigger market on Sundays in Floriana. ✎ *Triq Il-Merkanti • Map J2*

Triq Ir-Repubblika/ Republic Street
Valletta's showcase avenue and the surrounding streets have its biggest concentration of shops. You'll find familiar British high-street names alongside souvenir and jewellery shops. ✎ *Map H3–J2*

Agenda Bookshop
This friendly shop is probably Malta's best for English-language books. Its stock ranges from Malta-related titles (covering everything from temples to cooking) to beach reading.
✎ *26 Triq Ir-Repubblika • Map H2*

Blush & Panic
A small and attractive vintage shop in the capital, Blush & Panic has a collection of hats, scarves and jewellery. This fashionable store offers genuine bargains. ✎ *Melita Street • Map H2*

Marks & Spencer
This outpost of the famed British store has fashion for men, women and children, a small food section (with a selection of international wines), and an airy café. ✎ *44 Triq It-Teatru L'Antik • Map J2*

J. Piccinino
Malta's largest women's swimwear retailer offers styles from tiny bikinis to classic black one-pieces. There are many branches across Malta, several of them in Valletta. ✎ *238–9 Triq Ir-Repubblika • Map J2*

L-Arka
This small fair-trade shop offers toys, crafts, food, books, jewellery and ornaments from all over the developing world. It is also a hotspot for information on the latest awareness-raising cultural events in Malta. ✎ *306 Triq San Pawl • Map J2*

C. Camilleri
This old-fashioned bakery has been selling scrumptious cakes, sweets and confectionery since 1843. Try the local almond pastries, or deliciously sticky doughnuts and iced buns.
✎ *49–51 Triq Il-Merkanti • Map J2*

Malta Crafts Centre
This is a good place to find such Maltese specialities as brightly coloured L-Imdina glass, delicate lace, and handmade woollen jumpers from Gozo.
✎ *Misraħ San Ġwann • Map H2*

Heritage Malta Giftshop
This large, well-stocked shop at the entrance to the Museum of Archaeology sells its own comprehensive range of books, plus souvenirs and postcards.
✎ *Triq Ir-Repubblika • Map H2*

Right **Trabuxu** Right **The Pub**

🔟 Nightlife

1 Bridge Bar
Frequented by older patrons from the art world, this alfresco bar is particularly favoured on summer evenings. It also stages live music performances. ✪ *Triq Sant' Orsla • Map J3*

2 The Pub
This tiny hole-in-the-wall pub has a ghoulish claim to fame: it is here that Oliver Reed is said to have drunk himself to death during the filming of the movie *Gladiator*. Photos of the actor adorn the walls. ✪ *136 Triq L'Arcisoof • Map J2*

3 Trabuxu
Black-and-white photos of musical instruments cover the brick walls of this subterranean wine bar. Laid-back and stylish, it's a great spot to unwind after a hard day's sightseeing. ✪ *1 Triq Id-Dejqa • Map G4*

4 Streat
This bar is visited by the post-theatre crowd for whiskey and late-night snacks. It hosts parties that go on till the early morning hours. ✪ *Strait Street • Map J2*

5 Tico Tico
Vintage photographs adorn the walls of Tico Tico, an intimate lounge bar. It has a major role in helping a former red-light area earn a name for its thriving nightlife. ✪ *Strait Street • Map J2*

6 The Ordnance Pub
True Brit-pub atmosphere to be enjoyed in the heart of this Mediterranean capital: there's games on a large screen, beer on tap and good pub food too. ✪ *Ordnance Street • Map H2*

7 Legligin
An atmospheric wine bar offering a good range of local and international wines that can be enjoyed with a selection of Maltese nibbles. ✪ *119 Triq Santa Lucija • Map H2*

8 St James Cavalier Centre for Creativity
Valletta's vibrant arts centre offers a range of activities for the whole family, from cult-film screenings to theatre and dance performances *(see p40)*.

9 Mediterranean Conference Centre
Valletta's handsome conference centre, set in the atmospheric old hospital belonging to the Knights of St John, regularly hosts music, theatre, dance and other events, by local and overseas performers. ✪ *Triq Il-Mediterran • Map K2 • www.mcc.com.mt*

10 Manoel Theatre
This tiny jewel of a theatre makes for an atmospheric night out. Its stage has hosted some major international performers. The courtyard café is perfect for a light lunch *(see p66)*.

Left **Caffe Cordina** Right **Café Jubilee**

Cafés

1 Caffe Cordina
Valletta's most famous café, the elegant Cordina has a large, shady terrace on the square. The drinks and snacks (which include excellent *pastizzi*) are overpriced, but the location can't be beaten. *Misrah Ir-Repubblika • Map J2*

2 Inspirations
Part of the St James Cavalier Centre for Creativity *(see p40)*, Inspirations offers tasty Maltese and Italian dishes plus lighter fare such as soups and quiches. There's a pretty terrace. *Triq Papa Piju V • Map H3*

3 Café Jubilee
Small and wood-panelled, with tiny booths, this cosy spot is decorated with old posters. It is a favourite with locals working or shopping nearby, serving good sandwiches and light meals. *125 Triq Santa Lucija • Map H2*

4 Kantina Café
Located around the corner from St John's Co-Cathedral, this café serves good food and delicious cakes. It also has a substantial drinks menu. *St John's Square • Map J2*

5 Museum Café
Cluttered and cosy, with old prints and curios on the walls, this is a popular place for breakfast or a mid-morning snack. Try a creamy cappuccino and a couple of ricotta-filled *pastizzi*. *24 Triq Melita • Map H3*

6 Piadina Caffe
The place for healthy lunchtime snacks, Piadina's charming owner has made this a popular café. Great hot chocolate is served here *St Lucia Street • Map J3*

7 Café Deux Baronnes
An outdoor café with wrought-iron chairs and tables under crisp white parasols, the Café Deux Baronnes offers spectacular views over the whole of the Grand Harbour. *Upper Barrakka Gardens (lower level), Triq Sant' Ursula • Map H3*

8 Reno's Café
Ideal for a leisurely cup of coffee, Reno's is also the perfect spot for a quick bite or a light snack. *Ftira* (Maltese bread) with a filling of scrumptious items from the deli counter is recommended as a take away. *Zachary Street • Map H3*

9 Culto Caffetteria
Believed to serve one of the best coffees in Valletta, this tiny café also offers a wide selection of sandwiches and salads. *St John's Street • Map H2*

10 Café Manoel
This arty, fashionable café is tucked in the Manoel Theatre's courtyard. It serves sandwiches, home-made soups and classic local dishes such as rabbit stew. Opera plays in the background. *115 Triq It-Teatru L'Antik • Map J2*

Restaurants get busy at lunchtime so you may have to reserve a table then. In the evenings, you'll only have to book at weekends.

Price Categories

For a three-course	€ under €20
meal for one with half	€€ €20–€30
a bottle of wine (or	€€€ €30–€40
equivalent meal), taxes	€€€€ €40–€50
and extra charges.	€€€€€ over €50

Rubino Ristorante & Dolceria

🔟 Restaurants

Malata
Politicians and business people love this smart yet informal restaurant, which offers highly creative, beautifully prepared French fare. It overlooks the dancing fountains on St George's Square. ✎ *Misrah Il-Palazz • Map J2 • 2123 3967 • Closed Sun • €€€€*

Angelica
A wine bar, restaurant and café combined, Angelica is the place for anything from divine cupcakes to Maltese rabbit cooked in champagne. It's small, so booking is recommended. ✎ *134 Triq L-Arcisqof • Map J2 • 2122 2777 • Closed Sun • €€*

Giannini Ristorante
One of the finest restaurants in the capital, Giannini's offers sublime views to go with its sophisticated versions of local cuisine *(see p56)*.

Rubino Ristorante & Dolceria
A former confectioner's, Rubino's is a great place to try traditional local cooking. Desserts are still the highlight *(see p56)*.

Ambrosia
This coolly elegant eatery tucked down a side street serves creative and beautifully fresh local cuisine in a welcoming and informal atmosphere. Save room for the heavenly desserts. ✎ *137 Triq L-Arcisof • Map J2 • 2122 5923 • Closed Sun & public hols • €€*

Il Horza
This tiny Italian restaurant offers up delicious food and very friendly service. Options include seafood, beef and pasta dishes. There's an extensive list of Italian wines. ✎ *6 Triq San Kristofru • Map J2 • 2122 6936 • Closed Sun • €€€*

Black Pig
Enjoy extraordinary flavours at this restaurant that makes use of locally sourced, fresh produce. It has a regularly changing menu. ✎ *95 Old Bakery Street • Map J2 • 7922 1606 • €€€*

Crianza
This cheap and cheerful little pizza joint is in a cosy vaulted cellar. It serves pasta and salads as well as imaginatively topped pizzas. ✎ *33 Triq L'Arcisoof • Map J2 • 2123 8120 • Closed Sun L • €*

Sicilia
The dining room is tiny, but a terrace offers picture-postcard views over the Grand Harbour. Try the tasty pasta dishes or the fresh fish. Open lunchtimes only. ✎ *1A Triq San Gwann (above Victoria Gate) • Map J3 • 2124 0569 • Closed Mon–Sat D, Sun • €*

Palazzo Preca
Run by sisters Ramona and Roberta, Palazzo Preca is a fine-dining restaurant with a traditional ambience. Popular for its fish, it also serves delectable desserts. ✎ *54 Strait Street • Map H2 • 2122 6777 • Closed Mon • €€€*

Left **Armstrong 100-ton gun, Fort Rinella** Right **Spinola Bay, St Julian's**

Around Tas-Sliema, St Julian's and the Three Cities

VALLETTA'S CLOSE NEIGHBOURS – *Tas-Sliema and St Julian's to the northwest, the Three Cities (Il-Birgu/Vittoriosa, L-Isla/Senglea and Il-Kalkara) to the southeast – couldn't be more different. The Three Cities, piled on a pair of promontories jutting into the bay, are quiet, historic and time-worn, a far cry from the brash glitz of Tas-Sliema and St Julian's, where high-rise hotels, luxury apartments, shopping centres and neon-lit nightclubs have mushroomed.*

🔟 Sights

1. The Inquisitor's Palace, Il-Birgu
2. Collachio, Il-Birgu
3. Church of St Lawrence, Il-Birgu
4. Our Lady of Victories Church, L-Isla
5. Fort Rinella, Il-Kalkara
6. Paċeville
7. Fort St Angelo, Il-Birgu
8. Malta Maritime Museum, Il-Birgu
9. Triq It-Torri, Tas-Sliema
10. Spinola Bay, St Julian's

Gardens of the Inquisitor's Palace

1 The Inquisitor's Palace, Il-Birgu

In the late 1500s, word of the lax and frivolous lifestyle of the Knights in Malta reached the ears of the Pope in Rome. An Inquisitor was dispatched to the islands, with orders to bring the Knights to heel. This palace was not simply the Inquisitor's residence; it also served as court and prison. But today there is little sense of its former magnificence, or even of its former role. Only some 17th-century murals, a few cells, and the grand staircase survive. The Judgement Room strikes the only chilling note: prisoners entered the Inquisitor's presence through a half-sized door, forcing even the most defiant to bow.
○ Triq Il-Mina L-Kbira • Map L5 • 2182 7006 • 9am–5pm daily • Adm charge • www.heritagemalta.org

2 Collachio, Il-Birgu

Collachio is the area of Il-Birgu where the Knights built their auberges (inns) when they first arrived in Malta in the 1530s. This cool stone maze remains the most atmospheric district in the Three Cities, a place to abandon the map and lose yourself in the

Collachio

Our Lady of Victories Church, L-Isla

drowsy lanes. None of the auberges are currently open to the public, although the Auberge de France – now the Museum of the Maltese Language – may take visitors by prior arrangement. Very little has survived from the time of the Normans in Malta, but look out for an exquisitely carved Siculo-Norman window in the crumbling but picturesque old mansion at 11 Triq It-Tramuntana.
○ Map L5

3 Church of St Lawrence, Il-Birgu

A church has stood on this site for 900 years. The present elegant Baroque church was built by Lorenzo Gafa in 1681, and, after substantial bomb damage during World War II, has been lovingly restored (see p38).

4 Our Lady of Victories Church, L-Isla

This church remains close to the hearts of the Maltese, thanks to two much-venerated statues: the jewel-encrusted 17th-century statue of our Blessed Lady of Victories, and a statue of Christ the Redeemer which is widely believed to have miraculous healing powers (see p38).

The Lookout

Out at the very tip of L-Isla, the gardens of Ġnien Il-Gardjola contain a small but much-photographed *vedette* (lookout). Jutting out over the heights of Senglea Point, it frames a beautiful view of the Grand Harbour. The *vedette* is famously carved with symbols of vigilance: an eye, an ear and a crane. These were supposed to remind the sentries of their duty of watchfulness. The *vedette* was carefully dismantled and stored before World War II, and thus survived the bombs.

Fort Rinella, Il-Kalkara

Rinella was one of a pair of coastal batteries built in the 1880s by the British, against threats from Italy. It was equipped with a huge Armstrong 100-ton gun, but the introduction of quick-firing guns only 20 years later rendered this mighty weapon obsolete. A group of enthusiastic young men in Victorian garb stage an "animated tour" – letting off cannons, firing muskets and signalling furiously – to provide an enjoyable insight into the fort's history. (The 100-ton gun itself has only been fired once in recent years, causing the fort's ceilings to crack, so it now remains silent.)
◈ *Triq Santu Rokku • Map E4 • 2180 9713 • 10am–5pm Tue–Sun; animated tour 2:30pm • Adm charge • www.wirtartna.org*

Paċeville

Paċeville comprises a handful of small streets and alleys packed with bars, clubs and restaurants. On Saturday nights, the area is thronged with party people, both Maltese and tourists, all dressed to kill. Your feelings about Paċeville will probably depend on your age and notions of what constitutes a good holiday. All those under 25 in search of booze, bright lights and bars will find Paċeville the answer to every hedonistic dream. Everyone else will feel more comfortable in nearby St Julian's and Spinola Bay, where the restaurants and bars are geared towards an older and calmer clientele. ◈ *Map N1*

Fort St Angelo, Il-Birgu

This mighty fortress dominates the theatrical sweep of the Grand Harbour. Perhaps nothing evokes the drama of the Great Siege of 1565 like its imposing bulk when viewed from across the water in Valletta. Seat of the Grand Master until Valletta, the Knights' new capital, was constructed, it was here that punishment was meted out. Most feared was the "oubliette" – a pit hollowed out of the rock where wrongdoers were abandoned to the darkness and their own demons. The fortress withstood the Turks in 1565 and the German bombs in the 1940s. It is now closed to the public. ◈ *Map K4*

Paċeville nightlife

Fort St Angelo

8 Malta Maritime Museum, Il-Birgu

The grand 19th-century building overlooking Il-Birgu's seafront was built by the British to house the naval bakery. Now it contains a museum celebrating Malta's seafaring tradition *(see p41)*.

9 Triq It-Torri, Tas-Sliema

Tas-Sliema, once a fishing village and modest resort, is now a dense concrete jungle packed with hotels, shops, restaurants and bars. But some old-fashioned traditions have survived – notably the *passeggiata*, the traditional evening stroll imported from Italy. Each evening, couples and families amble along the seafront, Triq It-Torri (Tower Rd), nodding to neighbours and sizing up strangers. Pavement cafés make people-watching easier. The stretch from Għar Id-Dud to St Julian's Point is the most popular. ◈ *Map P2, Q2*

10 Spinola Bay, St Julian's

There is little natural beauty in the concrete sprawl of Malta's northern coast, but Spinola Bay, with its smattering of pretty villas, is a welcome exception. The small bay has become one of the most fashionable addresses in Malta. A clutch of smart restaurants with terraces overlook the bay. Multicoloured *luzzus* sway gently in the sun, as fishermen by the water's edge mend their nets. The bay is prettiest at night, when the twinkling lights are reflected in the water. ◈ *Map N1*

A Walk around the Three Cities

Morning

🕐 Enter **Il-Birgu** through its mighty main gate (where there is a very nice outdoor café for a coffee break) and head along Triq Il-Mina l-Kbira. On the right, you'll come to the **Inquisitor's Palace**, where unfortunate prisoners were accused of heresy. Behind the Inquisitor's Palace is the original Knights' quarter, called the **Collachio**. Head down Triq H. Tabone to see the **auberges** (inns) of the Knights, before returning to the central square, Misraħ Ir Rebħ. Turn right onto the Vittoriosa Waterfront and enjoy delicious food at any of the several good restaurants: an ideal place to catch beautiful views of yachts moored in the marina.

Afternoon

Wind your way down to the water's edge at Dockyard Creek. The **Freedom Monument**, in front of the splendid **Church of St Lawrence** commemorates those who died during World War II. Take a boat tour around the **Grand Harbour** (there are regular departures from the waterfront in Il-Birgu) for sublime views of Valletta and the Three Cities. Continue your stroll around the bay, following the water's edge to the entrance to **L-Isla**. Walk down L-Isla's main street, Triq Il-Vitorja, to the gardens right at the tip of the promontory; here you will find the famous *vedette* (**lookout**) with its curious symbols, offering more magnificent views.

St Julian's is a direct translation of San Ġiljan; its name was anglicized in the 19th century. Both names are used equally today.

Left **Plaza Shopping Mall** Right **The Point**

Shopping

1 Bay Street Mall, St Julian's

This stylish mall has branches of all the major chains (including most British and Italian high-street names), plus cafés, restaurants and kids' play areas. ◈ *St George's Bay • Map D3*

2 Plaza Shopping Mall, Tas-Sliema

Tas-Sliema's main shopping mall has high-street chains like Body Shop and Benetton, along with cafés and a well-stocked bookshop, Agenda. ◈ *Triq Bisazza • Map Q3*

3 Books Plus, Tas-Sliema

A wide variety of books on Malta, as well as works for children, fiction and non-fiction titles, are available in this bookstore spread over two floors. ◈ *Bisazza Street • Map Q3*

4 CamilleriParisMode, Tas-Sliema

Located close to the seafront, this elegant shop is known for the aesthetic quality of its products. A host of items ranging from home accessories to international delicacies are available here. ◈ *Annunciation Square • Map Q3*

5 The Point, Tas-Sliema

Located in the modern Tigne Point, Malta's largest mall offers a wide variety of stores including many British high-street names. ◈ *Tigne Point • Map E4*

6 Gadget Gadget, Tas-Sliema

An ideal place to find unique pieces of decor for the house, this shop also has cards and interesting gift options. ◈ *2a Triq San Duminku • Map Q3*

7 Bisazza Street, Tas-Sliema

As well as the Plaza Shopping Centre *(see left)* and a supermarket, all the usual high-street chains can be found on or around Bisazza Street, including Next, Mango and dozens more. ◈ *Map Q3*

8 Pedigree Toyshops, St Julian's

This branch of one of Malta's biggest toy retailers has all you need to keep young kids happy indoors, on the beach, or on the plane. It's also a good back-up on a rainy day. ◈ *Bay Street Tourist Complex, Level 0, St George's Bay • Map D3*

9 Diamonds International, St Julian's

Choose from diamonds, pearls, gold, silver and a plethora of other options offered at Malta's largest jewellery shop. ◈ *Portomaso • Map N1*

10 Tower Stores, Tas-Sliema

Village shops and fruit-and-vegetable vans supply most visitors' needs, but occasionally a supermarket comes in useful. There are now many in Malta; this is the biggest in this area. ◈ *Triq Ir-Kbira • Map Q3*

Left **Juuls** Right **Dragonara Palace Casino**

🔟 Nightlife

Places Club, Paceville

Popular among young-sters, this club has the perfect ambience for a party and holds special events on Friday nights. Lucrative offers at the bar pull in a bigger crowd. Commercial House is played more than any other genre of music. 🟢 *Ball Street • Map D3*

Qube, Paceville

Open till 4am daily, this themed bar has 60 brands and offers myriad flavours, with vodka being the preferred drink. Special promotions are held here on Wednesdays. 🟢 *Triq Ball • Map N1*

Coconut Grove, Paceville

Brash and noisy, this is a huge hit with local teenagers (it's strictly for the under-20s). To fit in, dress to impress – boys as well as girls. For full-blown heavy metal, try Remedy, the upstairs bar, on Friday and Saturday nights. 🟢 *Triq Wilġa • Map N1*

Havana Club, Paceville

One of the best clubs for R&B, soul and hip-hop on the island, situated in the heart of Paceville. 🟢 *Triq San Ġorġ • Map D3*

Level 22, St Julian's

A sophisticated bar frequented by an international crowd, Level 22 occupies a spectacular location on the top floor of the Portomaso Tower. 🟢 *Portomaso • Map N1*

Juuls, St Julian's

A characterful, cosy reggae club serving cocktails and fresh fruit juices and playing the best reggae, roots, dub and ragga on the islands. 🟢 *57 Joseph Street, Spinola Bay • Map N1*

Hugo's Passion, Paceville

In the centre of Paceville, this club sits atop the massively popular Hugo's Lounge. Let out the party animal in you on the dance floor, then unwind in the sofa lounge or at the outdoor tables. 🟢 *Triq San Ġorġ • Map D3*

Portomaso Casino, St Julian's

Frequented by both locals and foreigners and set below the Portomaso Tower, this casino offers options such as blackjack, slots and roulette. It also has the largest poker room in Malta. 🟢 *Portomaso • Map N1*

Dragonara Palace Casino, St Julian's

This 19th-century palazzo by the sea is Malta's most lavish casino, with gaming tables, slot machines and live entertainment. Dress smartly and take ID – it's for over-18s only. 🟢 *Dragonara Point • Map E3*

Eden SuperBowl and Cinemas, St Julian's

Malta's biggest cinema complex-cum-bowling alley has 16 screens showing Hollywood's best, plus an IMAX cinema. 🟢 *St George's Bay • Map D3*

Around Tas-Sliema, St Julian's and the Three Cities

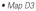 *Take note: nightclubs in Malta change names or close down with alarming frequency.*

Left **Café Giorgio** Right **Vinotheque Wine & Cheese Bar**

🔟 Bars and Cafés

1 Marina Terrace, St Julian's
Enjoy a brunch, lunch or an afternoon snack at this pizzeria and brasserie overlooking the pretty Portomaso Marina. A wide variety of wraps, burgers and sandwiches are served here. Outdoor seating is available and it also offers free Wi-Fi facility.
◈ *Portomaso • Map N1*

2 Cara's Café, Tas-Sliema
Popular with tourists and local workers alike, this bustling café has a great location on Tas-Sliema's seafront promenade. It serves snacks and light meals, but the cakes are the real high-light. ◈ *249 Triq It-Torri • Map P2*

3 Café Giorgio, Tas-Sliema
The perfect people-watching spot on Tas-Sliema's seafront. Soak up the evening sun on the terrace while the Maltese stroll past during their *passeggiata*.
◈ *Triq Ix-Xatt Tigne • Map Q3*

4 Dubliners, St Julian's
Enjoy a delicious Sunday roast at this Irish-themed bar that serves draught beers, wines and spirits. It also hosts live music programmes regularly.
◈ *Spinola Bay • Map N1*

5 Saddles Bar, St Julian's
A long-established bar with a small terrace overlooking Spinola Square and the bay. Saddles is also a venue for regular club nights. ◈ *Spinola Bay • Map N1*

6 Café Cuba, Tas-Sliema
Frequented by the shopping crowd, this seafront café offers a variety of wines, beers and cocktails. The burgers served here are extremely popular.
◈ *Triq ix-Xatt • Map F3*

7 Del Borgo Wine Bar, Il-Birgu
This popular bar boasts an extensive wine list and a menu of local delicacies. A major highlight is the Maltese bread pudding.
◈ *27 Tramuntana, Il-Birgu • Map L5*

8 Vinotheque Wine & Cheese Bar, St Julian's
This bright and breezy wine bar in a smart hotel offers an excellent array of local and overseas wines accompanied by light meals and snacks. There's a terrace for relaxing in summer. ◈ *Corinthia Marina Hotel, St George's Bay • Map D3*

9 Mint, Tas-Sliema
With an emphasis on fresh and healthy food, this family-friendly café offers a variety of options for vegetarians and people with special dietary needs. ◈ *Triq Windsor • Map Q2*

10 Il-Forn, Il-Birgu
Set in the heart of the old city, is a delightful wine bar and modern art gallery. It serves more than 100 wines and, in the evenings, Maltese dishes such as *ftira* (grilled bread), pasta, salads and mixed platters.
◈ *27 Triq Il-Tramutana • Map L5*

Raffael, St Julian's

Price Categories

For a three-course meal for one with half a bottle of wine (or equivalent meal), taxes and extra charges.

€ under €20
€€ €20–€30
€€€ €30–€40
€€€€ €40–€50
€€€€€ over €50

📭 Restaurants

1 Lupanaro, Il-Birgu
With the perfect setting for a romantic evening, this restaurant offers a feast of five specialities every night. ◎ *Vittoriosa Waterfront, Il-Birgu • Map K4 • 2180 3086 • €€*

2 Zest, St Julian's
This stylish restaurant offers contemporary continental and Asian cuisine. The open-air terrace bar is ideal for a pre-dinner drink. ◎ *25 St George's Rd • Map N1 • 2138 7600 • Closed Sun • €€€*

3 The Avenue, Paċeville
Kids love this hugely popular restaurant, which is brightly decorated in bold colours. It serves great pizzas and pasta at bargain prices. Book in advance or be prepared to queue. ◎ *Triq Gort • Map N1 • 2135 1753 • €€€*

4 L'Ordine, St Julian's
A traditional restaurant, L'Ordine recalls the era of the Knights, with its wrought-iron furniture and suits of armour. Enjoy fine Italian cuisine, and particularly good fresh fish. ◎ *47 Main Street, Balluta Bay • Map N2 • 2138 2923 • Closed Mon–Sat L • €€*

5 Barracuda, St Julian's
Set in a handsome villa leaning out over the water, this elegant and romantic restaurant is well-known for its superb seafood. Maltese dishes such as rabbit stew are also on the menu. ◎ *194 Main St, Balluta Bay • Map N2 • 2133 1817 • €€€€*

6 Raffael, St Julian's
Overlooking Spinola Bay, Raffael offers great salads, freshly prepared pizzas, home-made burgers and kebabs, and Maltese specialities. ◎ *Spinola Bay • Map N1 • 2135 2000 • €€€*

7 Cucina del-Sole, Tas-Sliema
Overlooking the Valletta bastions, this unassuming eatery serves delicious Mediterranean food in a beautiful setting. ◎ *Tigne Point • Map Q2 • 2060 3434 • €€€*

8 Tal-Petut, Il-Birgu
Chef Donald creates a private dining experience at Tal-Petut by formulating a separate menu for each customer. Reservations should be made in advance. ◎ *20 Triq P. Scicluna • Map L5 • 7942 1169 • €€*

9 Peppino's, St Julian's
Brick walls, sea views and check tablecloths set the tone of the smart restaurant upstairs, but the cosy wine bar downstairs is better value. Book early for an outdoor table. ◎ *31 Triq San Ġorġ • Map N1 • 2137 3200 • Closed Sun • €€ (wine bar), €€€ (restaurant)*

10 Blue Elephant, St Julian's
This romantic restaurant serves the finest Thai cuisine in Malta. Dine on the terrace overlooking the marina, or enjoy the lavish rainforest decor inside. ◎ *Hilton Hotel, Portomaso • Map N1 • 2138 3383 • Closed L daily • €€€€*

Left **Għadira Wetland Reserve** Right **Baħar Iċ-Ċagħaq**

Around Northern Malta

NORTHERN MALTA HAS AN UNUSUALLY DIVERSE RANGE *of attractions. Some of the island's boldest and brashest resorts can be found here – in particular the summer party capital of Buġibba. St Paul's Bay and the resort of Il-Mellieħa are somewhat quieter, appreciated by families and older visitors alike. The golden sands at Mellieħa Bay are the most popular on the island, but there are plenty of other*

beaches to choose from. If the kids ever get bored of the sun, sea and sand, note that Malta's top family attractions are clustered here – from water parks to the Popeye Village film set. Then there's a wilder side of Malta: stunning cliff walks, extraordinary coastal scenery and remote coves, especially along the western end of Marfa Ridge. For wild Malta of a different kind, visit the Għadira Wetland Reserve. Last but not least, there's ancient Malta, represented by the Skorba and Ta Ħaġrat Temples.

L-Imġarr

Sights

1. Il-Mellieħa
2. Għadira Wetland Reserve
3. St Paul's Bay
4. Buġibba and Qawra
5. Baħar Iċ-Ċagħaq (White Rocks)
6. Marfa Ridge
7. Popeye Village, Anchor Bay
8. L-Imġarr
9. Skorba Temples
10. Ta' Ħaġrat Temple

Preceding pages **The patterned interior of the Church of Santa Marija Assunta, Il-Mosta – generally known as Mosta Dome** *(see p85)*

St Paul's Bay

dominates the ornithological year, so the birds you see at this reserve will depend very much on the season. ◈ Il-Ghadira, Mellieha Bay • Map A2 • 2134 7646 • Buses 41, 42, 221, 222 • Open Nov–May: 10:30am–4:30pm Sat–Sun • Free (but donations accepted) • www.birdlifemalta.org

Il-Mellieħa

The family resort of Il-Mellieħa sprawls on a ridge overlooking the curve of Mellieħa Bay (see p46). It's a large resort, but remains fairly low-key, except during the mad months of July and August. Although Il-Mellieħa was one of the first parishes in Malta, the original 15th-century settlement proved too hard to defend from pirates and was soon abandoned. Now its raison d'être is tourism, and holiday-makers are drawn by the attractive sandy strip in the bay. Look out for the little shrine of Our Lady of Mellieħa. ◈ Map B2

Għadira Wetland Reserve

The illegal hunting and trapping of birds in Malta (see p111) has long caused international outrage. This wetland reserve, set just behind the sandy beach at Il-Mellieħa, was established as a haven for migrating birds by BirdLife, the local chapter of an international conservation group. They have gained considerable support from the people of Malta over the last few years, and a second reserve, near Xemxija, has also opened. Open days and family days are regularly organized, and volunteers give guided tours of the reserve at weekends. In Malta, more than almost anywhere else, migration

St Paul's Bay

The prettiest of the resorts around the bay of the same name, St Paul's Bay retains some vestiges of the salty old fishing cove from which it developed. It has no beaches, but there are some stretches of flat rocks on which to sunbathe (see p46).

Buġibba and Qawra

Big, brash Buġibba and its marginally quieter neighbour Qawra are two of the islands' largest resorts. Both are geared essentially towards the package tourism market; in summer, most of the hotels are block-booked by tour operators. Buġibba has the greatest concentration of nightlife, so you might get a better night's sleep in Qawra. Both offer lidos, boat trips and water sports. It can be hard to get around without your own transport, but you can take excursions if you don't want to hire a car. ◈ Map C3

Buġibba

Marfa Ridge

5 Baħar Iċ-Ċagħaq (White Rocks)

It's difficult to understand why this small bay remains so popular with local Maltese families, since it's very close to the main road and there's no sandy beach. Since the establishment here of two – for Malta, at least – sizeable family attractions, Mediterraneo Marine Park and the Splash & Fun Park *(see p52)*, it's even more hectic, especially at weekends and in summer. It's served by ice-cream and snack vans in summer, and there are cafés in both of the fun parks. ® *Map D3*

St Paul in Malta

According to legend, Saint Paul was shipwrecked in AD 60 in the bay now known as St Paul's Bay. He was attacked by a poisonous viper but, to the astonishment of the local people, survived completely unhurt. (A waspish Maltese saying suggests that when the venom left Malta's vipers, it entered the tongues of Maltese women.) St Paul went on to convert the Roman governor Publius to Christianity, and appointed him first bishop of Malta. There are numerous sites dedicated to the saint throughout the islands, all the focus of intense devotion and pilgrimage.

---

6 Marfa Ridge

On a map, the Marfa Ridge looks like a fish's tail tacked onto the round body of the island. The main landmarks are the storybook crenellations of the Red Tower and the towering cliffs of Ras Il-Qammieħ. The coastline is pitted with numerous coves and beaches, and the whole area is a paradise for walkers *(see pp43, 45)*.

7 Popeye Village, Anchor Bay

Anchor Bay was originally named after the scores of stone Roman anchors that washed up there. Since 1980, it has been known for a Hollywood film set – the Popeye Village *(see p52)*.

Popeye Village

8 L-Imġarr

There are two places called L-Imġarr in the Maltese islands: the harbour in Gozo where the ferry arrives, and this sleepy little village on the island of Malta. The locals' pride and joy is the "Egg Church", built in the 1930s with funds raised by the sale of eggs. You can also explore an underground shelter used during World War II, where the rooms have been refurbished to look as they would have during the bombardment of Malta in the

1940s. L-Imġarr is a good place to try the typically Maltese dish of *fenek*, or rabbit, cooked in various ways *(see p54)*. The important Ta' Ħaġrat and Skorba temples *(see below)* are also in the vicinity. ◈ Map B3

Skorba Temples

The Skorba Temples at Żebbieħ, along with those at Ġgantija on Gozo *(see p35)* are believed to be among the oldest freestanding structures in the world. Excavations have unearthed even earlier shrines in the same location. Although the site has provided significant information for archaeologists there is surprisingly little to see. Look out for holes, bored into the paving slabs at the entrance. Many of the temples have this feature; it has been suggested that the blood of sacrificed animals was poured down the holes to propitiate the gods. The site looks its best in spring, when the countryside is green and lush *(see p34)*.

Ta' Ħaġrat Temple

This temple, near L-Imġarr, was probably linked in ancient times to those at Skorba, about 1 km (half a mile) away. It was first excavated in the 1920s under the direction of the Maltese scholar Sir Themistocles Zammit, with the help of the local community. There is little to see, but the rural setting is very attractive *(see p34)*.

Skorba Temples

A Drive around Northern Malta

Morning

🕐 This trip starts from and ends at **Il-Mellieħa**. If the nearby **Ghadira Wetland Reserve** is open, take one of the fascinating guided tours around this sanctuary for wetland birds. This is especially recommended during the spring and autumn migratory seasons. Otherwise, head west to **Popeye Village** for an enjoyable tour around the old film set. Have a quick dip in the sea at the tiny beach. Take the main road from Il-Mellieħa up to the **Marfa Ridge**. Stop by the Red Tower to enjoy the views of Gozo and Comino, then continue to **Ras Il-Qammieħ** (Qammieħ Point) to see the spectacular cliffs. Return to Il-Mellieħa on the main road, and continue to **St Paul's Bay**. Have a lazy 🍴 lunch overlooking the bay at **Gillieru**.

Afternoon

Follow the road for 4 km (2 miles) through the fertile **Pwales Valley**, with its green fields girdled by tumbling stone walls. Park at the top of the cliff and make the descent via almost two hundred stone steps to **Għajn Tuffieħa** beach. Stretch out and work on your tan for a couple of hours. If you are feeling more active, you could hike around the headland to the busier bay at **Golden Beach**, or perhaps take a boat trip to the quiet cove at **Fomm Ir-Riħ**. The little village of **L-Imġarr** is famous for its old-fashioned Maltese cooking. Try some typical 🍴 local rabbit (or simply a drink) at the Friend-to-All Bar on the village square.

Left **Għajn Tuffieħa Bay** Right **Fomm Ir-Riħ Bay**

TOP 10 Beaches and Bays

1 Paradise Bay
A snug bay with a crescent of sand reached by a flight of steps cut into the rock. It's a very popular spot, best during the week or out of season. Bring your snorkel. ◈ *Map A2*

2 Għajna Bay
This is a picturesque bay with a small stretch of sand in the middle of a wide arc of flat rocks, backed by creamy limestone cliffs. A handful of boathouses overlook tiny coves. It's a favourite with local families. ◈ *Map A3*

3 Għajn Tuffieħa Bay
A beautiful bay set against terraced hills, with wonderful cliff walks stretching off in either direction *(see p46)*.

4 Golden Bay
This sandy beach is easily accessible and offers several amenities including canoe and pedalo rental. The beach is subject to dangerous currents from time to time; don't swim if the red flag is flying. ◈ *Map A3*

5 Mellieħa Beach
It's hard to believe, but this narrow crescent of shoreline is Malta's largest sandy beach. Unfortunately, it's backed by a main road, but this and its location make it easy to reach by bus or car. It's very popular with families, and has excellent amenities *(see p46)*.

6 Little Armier
There are two Armier beaches – Armier and Little Armier. The first is scruffy and rather unappealing, but the latter is a sandy little cove with a basic beach café. ◈ *Map B2*

7 Salina Bay
The broad sweep of Salina Bay is lined with hotels and apartment blocks. Although there is no beach as such, the flat rocks are good for sunbathing, and the shallow waters are perfect for a dip. The bay gets its name from the nearby salt pans. ◈ *Map C3*

8 Mistra Bay
It's easy to miss the turning for this delightful little strand near Xemxija: a country road scented with honeysuckle leads to the narrow bay where the swimming and snorkelling are good and relatively undisturbed. ◈ *Map B2*

9 Fomm Ir-Riħ Bay
This wild and beautiful beach is difficult to get to; as a result few people make it here except in the very height of summer *(see p44)*.

10 Anchor Bay
This pretty little cove next to the touristy Popeye Village *(see p52)* somehow gets overlooked by the crowds. The sandy beach is little larger than a handkerchief, but it's a good spot for a picnic. ◈ *Map A3*

Price Categories

For a three-course meal for one with half a bottle of wine (or equivalent meal), taxes and extra charges.

€	under €20
€€	€20–€30
€€€	€30–€40
€€€€	€40–€50
€€€€€	over €50

Il-Veċċja Restaurant & Wine Bar

TOP 10 Restaurants

1 The Arches, Il-Mellieħa
Lovely and light-filled, with a small covered terrace, The Arches serves some of Malta's best French cuisine. The service and wine list are excellent. ✪ *113 Triq Gorg Borg Olivier • Map B3 • 2152 3460 • Closed Mon–Sat L, Sun • €€€*

2 Gillieru, St Paul's Bay
A large, family-friendly place with a perfect setting overlooking the bay, Gillieru is good for lunch, dinner or just a coffee break. Try the ultra-fresh fish. ✪ *66 Triq Il-Knisja • Map C3 • 2157 3480 • €€€*

3 Friend-to-All Bar
Three L-Imġarr bars are known for traditional rabbit dishes. This simple spot is perhaps the friendliest and certainly the cheapest. Rabbit, cooked various ways, is all that's on the menu. ✪ *L-Imġarr village square • Map B3 • 2157 3235 • Closed Sun, Mon L • €*

4 Il-Mithna, Mellieħa
Innovative fusion food is served with a Maltese twist at this restaurant that was originally a 17th-century mill. It also offers the option of alfresco dining. ✪ *58 Main Street • Map B3 • 2152 0404 • Closed daily L • €€€€*

5 Giuseppi's Restaurant & Wine Bar, Il-Mellieħa
Traditional dishes are given a contemporary twist. Locals rave about rabbit with bitter chocolate sauce. ✪ *25 Triq Sant' Elena • Map B3 • 2158 6401 • Closed L, Sun • €€€*

6 The Whole Hog
Popular for its giant sandwiches, this gastro-pub with an English ambience, serves delicious Sunday roasts. ✪ *Tourist Street • Map C3 • 9995 3234 • €€*

7 Paukus Dining, Bugibba
Frequented by fish lovers, this restaurant is famous for the freshness of its catch. One of the highlights here is the Tuscan/Maltese fish soup and seafood platter. ✪ *49 Bognor Street • Map C3 • 7755 1102 • €€*

8 Il-Veċċja Restaurant & Wine Bar, St Paul's Bay
A characterful 18th-century inn perched beside the harbour. Highlights include fresh fish and Maltese rabbit stew. ✪ *372 Triq San Pawl • Map C3 • 2158 2376 • Closed Mon–Sat L & Sun D in winter • €€€*

9 Xatba, Il-Mellieħa
Rich pasta and risotto dishes, perfectly prepared fresh fish and grilled meats are served at this family-run restaurant, a favourite with locals and tourists. ✪ *Triq Il-Marfa • Map B2 • 2152 1753 • Closed L daily • €€*

10 Ganesha Restaurant, Xemxija
Classical dishes from all over India are featured here, with host Bernice and her staff ready to help guide you through the menu. ✪ *Triq L'Imgiebah, Xemxija Heights • Map B3 • 2157 2202 • €€*

Left **L-Imdina** Right **"Clapham Junction"** Cart Ruts

Around Central Malta

POISED ON A PLATEAU IN THE VERY CENTRE OF THE ISLAND, *L-Imdina* is Malta's ancient capital and its most beautiful city. Its streets are charged with history, and, particularly after dusk, each faded palace and medieval chapel seems to whisper its secrets. Nearby Ir-Rabat is just as old and has a special place in the hearts of the devout Maltese: it was here that St Paul

was supposedly brought after the shipwreck in AD 60. To the south, the gorgeous Dingli Cliffs are perfect for hiking and picnicking, with fine views, while the shady Buskett Gardens offer respite from the summer heat, and the Bronze Age cart ruts of "Clapham Junction" remain mysterious. Il-Mosta is dominated – as is much of the island – by the enormous dome of its parish church, which miraculously escaped destruction during World War II.

Verdala Palace and Buskett Gardens

🔟 Sights

1	L-Imdina
2	Ir-Rabat
3	Dingli Cliffs
4	Mosta Dome, Il-Mosta
5	"Clapham Junction" Cart Ruts, Msierah
6	Verdala Palace and Buskett Gardens
7	Palazzo Parisio, In-Naxxar
8	Fort Madliena, Madliena
9	The Three Villages (Hal Balzan, Hal Lija, H'Attard)
10	San Anton Palace Gardens, H'Attard

L-Imdina

L-Imdina dreams quietly behind her impenetrable walls. Time stopped for the ancient capital when the seafaring Knights arrived in the 1530s, settling around the Grand Harbour – and sidelining L-Imdina and its people in the process. "The Silent City", as it is still known, may fill up with tourists by day, but the hush returns with nightfall when the crowds depart. If you can, explore this lovely city by day, and again by night (see pp16–17).

Ir-Rabat

Ir-Rabat and L-Imdina were once a single entity, before the Arabs walled and fortified L-Imdina almost a thousand years ago. Ir-Rabat retains the islands' most evocative Roman remains in its Domus Romana. The remnants of this once opulent Roman villa are beside a small museum containing fine mosaics and frescoes from the

Rabat – St Agatha and St Paul

Roman era. Many of Malta's most resonant religious sites are concentrated in Ir-Rabat. They include the grotto where St Paul is said to have lived after he was shipwrecked, catacombs dating back to the very early years of Christianity and a cave painted with 14th-century murals where St Agatha is said to have hidden (see pp16–17).

Dingli Cliffs

Dingli Cliffs

The spectacular Dingli Cliffs are wild and undeveloped – a rare treat on the crowded little island of Malta. They provide the perfect terrain for walking and picnics, with fine views out to little Filfla Island (see p43).

Mosta Dome, Il-Mosta

It's impossible to miss the gigantic dome of Il-Mosta's parish church, which is visible from much of the island. Once the third-largest dome in Europe, it was relegated to fourth place in 1971 when the Xewkija Rotunda in Gozo was completed – at least according to the Gozitans. The people of Il-Mosta insist that their dome beats that of Ix-Xewkija when measured by volume rather than by height (see p38).

"Clapham Junction" Cart Ruts, Msierah

Mysterious Bronze Age grooves have been found across Malta, but this is the most dramatic site, with thousands of tracks etched into the rock on a wild and beautiful plateau near the Dingli Cliffs. Although they are called cart ruts, no one really knows what they are (see p35).

Mosta Dome

The Miracle at Il-Mosta

A congregation of about three hundred had gathered for Mass on the afternoon of 9 April 1942 when a German bomb pierced the lofty Mosta Dome, clattered onto the floor and skidded through the church. Unbelievably, the bomb didn't explode, and the Maltese have always chosen to interpret this as a miracle. You can see a replica of the bomb, along with some period photographs of the church during World War II, in a small museum which is part of the church.

6 Verdala Palace and Buskett Gardens

Visible from much of southern Malta, the crenellated turrets of Verdala Palace seem to float above dense forest. The palace was built as a summer residence for Grand Master Hughes de Verdalle in 1588, but it is now used by the Maltese president and is not open to the public. The forest, known as the Buskett Gardens (see p43), constitutes Malta's only real woodlands, with leafy paths and picnic areas. ◈ Triq Il-Buskett • Map C5

Palazzo Parisio

7 Palazzo Parisio, In-Naxxar

This aristocratic palace was originally built for the popular Portuguese Grand Master Manoel de Vilhena (see p36) in 1733. At the end of the 19th century, it was bought by a noble Maltese family, who completely transformed their new acquisition. The result was an opulent mansion which combined all the latest fashions (including the telephone) with superb local craftsmanship. Don't miss the beautiful formal Baroque gardens, elegant and particularly lovely in spring (see pp18–19).

8 Fort Madliena, Madliena

This sturdy, pentagonal fort was one of four built to defend the Victoria Lines. The 12-km (7-mile) walls and their fortifications were built by the British in the late 19th century and completely spanned the island east to west. Fort Madliena still commands the surrounding countryside from its lofty promontory on Malta's northeastern coast, and is the only one of the four open to visitors. Best of all are the views out over the old fortified walls, which spill down a steep gorge – overgrown now but still surprisingly intact. The fort is run by the St John Rescue Corps, which puts on guided tours at weekends. ◈ Map D3 • 7928 3333 • Tours by appointment

9 The Three Villages (Ħal Balzan, Ħal Lija, Ħ'Attard)

These villages consist of three neighbouring settlements. At first glance, they blend blandly into the suburban sprawl that extends dustily over much of Malta. And yet their historic kernels contain some of the island's most desirable addresses. Safe from the Ottomans after the Great Siege of 1565, the Maltese began a building boom, and the smartest

Fort Madliena

villas and palaces were built in the Three Villages. The villages grew, and their boundaries merged, but they remained fashionable under the British and even today. A wander through these affluent, leafy streets brings you face to face with medieval parish churches and Baroque villas, English-style mansions and contemporary luxury apartment blocks. The loveliest church is the 1613 parish church at Ħ'Attard, built by Tommaso Dingli and probably the finest Renaissance church on the islands. ◐ *Map C4, D4*

🔟 San Anton Palace Gardens, Ħ'Attard

These quiet and beautiful gardens are tucked away in San Anton, a hushed suburb of Ħ'Attard. The gardens are attached to a splendid summer palace, built by Grand Master Antoine de Paule in the 1620s. The palace is now the official residence of the President of Malta and is closed to visitors, but a section of the palace gardens has been open to the public since 1882. They are at their most beautiful in spring, when the carefully manicured flowerbeds and elegantly arranged flowerpots explode in a riot of colour and scent. A small aviary contains peacocks and other exotic birds. ◐ *De Paule Ave, San Anton • Map D4 • Open 8am–dusk*

A Walk in L-Imdina

Morning

🕐 Enter L-Imdina through the main gate. Almost immediately on the right, you'll pass the **Palazzo Vilhena** (now the Natural History Museum; *see p16*). Peek at the patio by the main entrance (the museum itself is rather dull) before heading to the sumptuous **Xara Palace Hotel** *(see p113)* for coffee in a marvellous 18th-century palace. Continue up narrow Triq San Pawl until you reach **St Paul's Cathedral** *(see p38)*, one of the most beautiful ecclesiastical buildings in Malta. Across the square, the **Cathedral Museum** *(see p41)* is an enjoyably chaotic treasure-trove of unexpected delights. The highlight is the collection of magnificent Dürer engravings and woodcuts. For lunch, try one of the cafés behind St Paul's Square.

Afternoon

Walk up **Triq Villegaignon** *(see p17)*, L-Imdina's finest street, lined with elaborate churches and graceful palaces with worn stone escutcheons. Look out for the **Casa Testaferrata** on the right; the French governor was thrown from the balcony of this noble house in 1798, when the Maltese decided they had had enough of the greedy French troops. Farther up, the **Palazzo Falson** is the best-preserved medieval palace in L-Imdina. Triq Villegaignon opens up into the **Pjazza Tas-Sur** (Bastion Square), where breathtaking views unfold of the whole of central Malta. Close by, the open-air **Fontanella Tea Gardens** *(see p89)* are a good stop for tea and cakes.

Left **Wignacourt Aqueduct** Centre **Ta' Qali Crafts Village** Right **Mk IX Spitfire, Malta Aviation Museum**

Best of the Rest

1 Limestone Heritage, Is-Siġġiewi

Malta is one huge quarry, the source of the stone that built the ancient temples and the city of Valletta. Audiovisual displays at this former quarry tell the story. ◈ Triq Mons M. Azzopardi • Map C5 • 2146 4931 • Open Mon–Fri 9am–3pm, Sat–Sun 9am–noon • Adm charge • www.limestoneheritage.com

2 Ta' Qali Crafts Village

Refurbished Nissen huts on a disused airfield showcase traditional Maltese crafts, from glass-blowing to pottery. There are demonstrations, and prices are reasonable. ◈ Ta' Qali airfield, between L-Imdina and H'Attard • Map C4 • Open Mon–Sat 9am–4pm • Free

3 Malta Aviation Museum

A fascinating collection of vintage aircraft, including a WWII Spitfire and Hurricane (see p53).

4 Ħal Qormi

An otherwise humdrum town, Ħal Qormi has two claims to fame: it makes the best bread in the islands, and it has one of the largest and most flamboyant Baroque churches, the Church of St George. ◈ Map D4

5 Birkirkara

One of the largest Maltese towns since medieval times, Birkirkara preserves a small and atmospheric old quarter and a pair of handsome parish churches. ◈ Map D4

6 Wignacourt Aqueduct, H'Attard

This 16-km (10-mile) aqueduct funded in 1610 by Grand Master Wignacourt was still bringing water from Ir-Rabat to Valletta more than two centuries later. A large section survives in H'Attard. ◈ Triq Peter Paul Rubens • Map C4

7 Victoria Lines

The Great Fault, a dramatic natural fissure, cuts across Malta east–west. It is a natural line of defence, which the British built on to form the Victoria Lines. It's great walking country. ◈ Map B4

8 Fort Mosta

One of four British-built forts which guarded the Victoria Lines, this well-preserved example of Victorian engineering was finished in 1879 but never saw battle. ◈ Map C3 • Open Mon for guided tours

9 San Pawl Tat-Tarġa (Cart Ruts)

These strange grooves cut into stone have puzzled historians for centuries. If they are cart ruts, why do they run off the edge of cliffs? If not, what are they? ◈ San Pawl Tat-Tarġa, near In-Naxxar • Map C3

10 Ħaż-Żebbuġ

A shabby triumphal arch hints at Ħaż-Żebbuġ's former glory. Its vast church, designed by Gerolamo Cassar, architect of St John's, Valletta, has fared better, and its elegant spires float above the town. ◈ Map C5

Price Categories

For a three-course meal for one with half a bottle of wine (or equivalent meal), taxes and extra charges.

€	under €20
€€	€20–€30
€€€	€30–€40
€€€€	€40–€50
€€€€€	over €50

De Mondion restaurant, Xara Palace Hotel, L-Imdina

🔟 Restaurants and Cafés

1 Fontanella Tea Gardens, L-Imdina

Perched on the ramparts behind L-Imdina's cathedral, Fontanella has spectacular views. Tea and cakes are served in an ivy-draped courtyard or out on the terrace. Service is famously bad. ✪ *1 Triq Is-Sur • Map C4 • 2145 4264 • €€*

2 Medina, L-Imdina

Medina's thick stone walls have stood for almost a thousand years. In summer, you can dine under vines in the courtyard. The menu fuses French, Italian and Mediterranean cuisines. ✪ *7 Triq Is-Salib Imqaddes • Map C4 • 2145 4004 • Closed Sun, Mon–Sat L • €€€€*

3 Fra Giuseppe, Hal Balzan

Situated in a former doctor's surgery, this café offers traditional Maltese fare. In summer, tables are available outside. ✪ *3 Triq Dun Spir Sammut, Hal Balzan • Map D4 • 2149 9440 • €€*

4 De Mondion, L-Imdina

One of Malta's few genuine gastronomic temples, De Mondion is located in one of its most beautiful hotels, the Xara Palace. Eat superb food in a romantic setting. ✪ *Xara Palace Hotel • Map C4 • 2145 0560 • Closed Sun, Mon–Sat L • €€€€€*

5 Trattoria AD 1530, L-Imdina

An array of pizza, pasta and salads are served throughout the day at this relaxed trattoria set in a beautiful square. ✪ *Xara Palace Hotel • Map C4 • 2145 0560 • €€€*

6 Rickshaw, Hal Balzan

One of Malta's best Far Eastern restaurants, it serves Oriental cocktails and has an impressive menu. ✪ *Corinthia Palace Hotel, De Paule Ave, Hal Balzan • Map D4 • 2144 0301 • Open 7–11pm Tue–Sat • €€€€*

7 Caffé Luna, In-Naxxar

This is one of Malta's favourite meeting places, serving delicious light lunches, traditional afternoon teas and all-day refreshments on the garden terraces or in the stylish interior. ✪ *Palazzo Parisio • Map C4 • 2141 2461 • Closed Sun–Tue D • €€€*

8 Bobbyland

Staggering views over the Dingli Cliffs are this country restaurant's main attraction. The food is simple country fare like rabbit and lamb. Avoid weekends, when it's jam-packed. ✪ *Triq l-Irdum, Had-Dingli • Map B5 • 2145 2895 • Closed Mon • €€*

9 L'Agape

Located off Rabat Square, L'Agape uses fresh, seasonal ingredients and has a menu that changes daily. ✪ *25 St Kataldu Street • Map C4 • 2099 2209 • €€*

10 Ir-Razzett l'Antik, Hal Qormi

Staff in period costume serve 18th-century cuisine at this friendly restaurant in a historic building filled with antiques and curios. ✪ *Valley Road • Map D4 • 2147 0221 • Closed Mon–Sat L, Sun L in winter • €€*

Ħaġar Qim and Mnajdra Temples

Around Southern Malta

SOUTHERN MALTA BOASTS the island's most exceptional ancient site in the underground necropolis of the Ħal Saflieni Hypogeum, as well as the two most picturesque temples at Ħaġar Qim and Mnajdra. It also has the prettiest fishing harbour (Marsaxlokk), most dramatic cave (the Blue Grotto) and loveliest medieval chapels (Old St Gregory's and Ħal Millieri). Quiet, low-key resorts such as Marsaskala are good for families, and there's some fine hiking and bathing to be done in the Delimara Peninsula. This southern corner of the island is rural and tranquil, with patchwork fields defined by old stone walls. Each peaceful little village has its own ornate Baroque church, which is the centre of village life, and is best seen when lit up for the village festa.

Sights

1. Ħaġar Qim and Mnajdra Temples
2. Ghar Dalam Cave and Museum, Birżebbuġa
3. Ħal Saflieni Hypogeum
4. Tarxien Temples
5. Marsaxlokk
6. Marsaskala
7. Blue Grotto, Wied Iż-Żurrieq
8. Ghar Lapsi
9. Delimara Peninsula
10. St John the Evangelist Chapel, Ħal Millieri, Iż-Żurrieq

Marsaxlokk

Preceding pages **View of L-Isla from Il-Birgu**

1 Hagar Qim and Mnajdra Temples

These two beautiful temples emerge from a sea of poppies on a clifftop overlooking the sea. Overgrown fields with tumbling limestone walls stretch in every direction, and the lonely location only adds to the charged atmosphere. The

Tarxien Temples

temples are made of soft globigerina limestone, which wind and time have eroded into lacy shapes. Renovations, now complete, should preserve the soft stone from further erosion. Both temples are fascinating; Hagar Qim is the largest and most complex, while Mnajdra seems to have been designed to act as a stone calendar *(see pp14–15)*.

2 Ghar Dalam Cave and Museum, Birżebbuġa

Ghar Dalam is a unique cave and prehistoric site, where a spectacular collection of 180,000-year-old bones belonging to long-extinct animals – which included dwarf hippopotamuses and dwarf elephants – were deposited at the end of the Ice Age. You can visit the cave, plus the small museum that is attached, where two rooms display the main finds of the palaeontologists *(see p35)*.

Figurine from the Hal Saflieni Hypogeum

Ghar Dalam Museum

3 Hal Saflieni Hypogeum

Malta's most astonishing ancient treasure, this vast, 5,000-year-old underground cemetery was hewn by hand from the rock. It was here that the famous sculpture of the "Sleeping Lady" was found *(see p40)*. If you see only one megalithic site in Malta, make it this one – but be sure to book your ticket well ahead *(see pp22–3)*.

4 Tarxien Temples

The Tarxien Temples are the most complex of Malta's temple sites, and include a cremation cemetery that was in use in the Bronze Age. Extensive prehistoric art and decorative objects have been found here, including part of a colossal human figure and beautiful spiral and animal reliefs. An altar containing a flint knife and animal bones suggests that offerings were made *(see p34)*.

5 Marsaxlokk

This is Malta's prettiest and most authentic fishing port. The delightful harbour is filled with bobbing, brightly coloured *luzzus*. Cobalt-blue fishing nets are spread out along the quays, and countless fish restaurants surround the bay *(see pp20–21)*.

For Old St Gregory's chapel **See p96**

The Not-So-Great Great White Shark

Little Wied Iż-Żurrieq made international news in 1987, when a local fisherman landed a huge great white shark. Locals claimed that it was 7 m (23 ft) long, which would have made it one of the biggest great whites ever discovered. (If you hear this story from your fisherman-guide on the way to the Blue Grotto, it's likely that it will have grown another metre or two.) Unfortunately, after scientists did tests with photographs, the shark's size was eventually revealed to be around 5–5.5 m (17–18 ft) – big, certainly, but no larger than many other great whites discovered in the Mediterranean.

Marsaskala

An overgrown fishing village that still retains its fishing fleet, Marsaskala has become one of the biggest resorts at the southern end of the island. Despite its size, it retains a sleepy charm, and even in July and August, when the town is crammed to the gills, it's still quieter and less frenzied than the northern resorts. Families stroll along the harbour front during the evening *passeggiata*, watching the fishermen mending their nets, before heading to one of the area's excellent seafood restaurants. For swimming and snorkelling, walk around the headland to nearby St Thomas's Bay, which is extremely popular with the Maltese although not especially attractive. ◈ *Map F5*

Blue Grotto, Wied Iż-Żurrieq

At the tiny cove of Wied Iż-Żurrieq, a straggle of café-bars and tourist shops have sprung up to cater for the streams of visitors on their way to see the fabled Blue Grotto. Walk along the cliff path or take a boat ride into the massive cave *(see p43)*.

Għar Lapsi

A natural lido formed by a rock pool scooped from the cliff, Għar Lapsi sounds much prettier than it is. The setting is quiet and attractive, but the pools are cursed with a coating of slimy seaweed and old rubbish. In spite of this, the Maltese adore Għar Lapsi and come in droves during the summer months, when the lively family atmosphere lends it a certain charm. Watching the comings and goings of the fishermen who also use the cove is a pleasant way to spend an afternoon. A couple of restaurants overlook the lido, and offer panoramic views over the coastline. ◈ *Map C6*

Delimara Peninsula

This finger of land is the site of a huge and unsightly power station. Yet, remarkably, the Delimara Peninsula is one of the prettiest corners in all Malta.

Marsaskala

Blue Grotto

Neat vegetable and flower plots are interspersed with stretches of wilder country with undulating fields, and there are wonderful swimming holes. The best of them is the pretty little cove of St Peter's Pool *(see p46)*, where the limestone cliffs have been eroded into ice-cream curves and the water is impossibly blue. There's another good spot for a swim at the very end of the peninsula, where the diving is particularly good. ✎ *Map F6*

St John the Evangelist Chapel, Hal Millieri, Iż-Żurrieq

This tiny, stone-built chapel near the tranquil little town of Iż-Żurrieq was built on the remnants of an older chapel and was consecrated in 1480. It was the parish church of Casal Millieri, an ancient village that has long since disappeared, leaving just the lonely chapel in its grove of lofty pines. Inside, the arched vault is divided into five bays, each beautifully decorated with frescoes depicting various saints, including St George enthusiastically finishing off the dragon. These frescoes were buried under layers of whitewash for many years and their bottom sections are irredeemably damaged. ✎ *Map D6*
• 2122 5952 • *Visits by appointment*
• *Free* • *www.dinlarthelwa.org*

A Tour around Southern Malta

Morning

🕐 Get to **Wied Iż-Żurrieq** early to avoid the queues for the **Blue Grotto**. It's at its best in the bright morning sunshine when the water is a vivid electric blue. After the boat trip, head to **Marsaxlokk** – a tricky drive because there are few signs. (Take the Ħal Kirkop–Il-Gudja–Ħal Għaxaq route to avoid getting lost in the Ħal Far industrial estate.) Once in the charming fishing port of Marsaxlokk, go for a stroll around the harbour and admire the multicoloured *luzzus* bobbing in the bay, before enjoying an alfresco lunch. For fresh seafood and harbour views, get a table on the water's edge at **Pisces** *(see p97)* but remember to book it well in advance.

Afternoon

After lunch, drive (or take a stroll) out to **St Peter's Pool** on the **Delimara Peninsula**. Fishermen will also ferry passengers from Marsaxlokk harbour to the little cove. Spend a couple of hours sunbathing and swimming in the pool's transparent waters. Then hop into the car for the short drive to **Marsaskala**, where you should just be in time to join the evening *passeggiata* around the harbour. Stop for a drink in one of the seafront cafés before pondering where to have dinner. To push the boat out, go for Grabiel *(see p57)*, which many consider to be the best seafood restaurant on the island.

Left **Old St Gregory's** Middle **St Catherine's** Right **Chapel of Our Lady of Graces**

🔟 Churches and Chapels

1 Chapel of Our Lady of Providence, near Is-Siġġiewi

This dainty octagonal chapel is usually closed, but through a window you may spot a cannon ball said to date from the Great Siege (1565). ⚲ *2 km (1 mile) from Is-Siġġiewi on Għar Lapsi road • Map C5 • 2146 0827 • Open for Mass 1 Sep*

2 St Nicholas, Is-Siġġiewi

Designed by the prestigious Baroque architect Lorenzo Gafa, this enormous, stately church dominates Is-Siġġiewi's central square. ⚲ *Pjazza San Nicolas • Map C5 • 2146 0827 • Festa last Sun in Jun*

3 Chapel of Our Lady of Graces, Ħaż-Żabbar

The pink, frilly domes of this Baroque church, also called the Żabbar Sanctuary, dominate the town's traffic-blighted old centre. A museum contains sailors' ex-votos. ⚲ *Triq Is-Santwarju • Map E5 • 2182 4383 • Festa first Sun after 8 Sep*

4 Our Lady of the Annunciation, Ħal Tarxien

This august 17th-century parish church sits serenely at the centre of a confusing maze of narrow streets. ⚲ *Triq Il-Kbira • Map E5 • 2182 8153 • Festa fifth Sun after Easter*

5 St Catherine's, Iż-Żejtun

The grandiose 17th-century parish church dominates this languid village. Designed by Lorenzo Gafa, it overlooks the square. ⚲ *Main square • Map E5 • 2169 4563 • Festa Jun (date varies)*

6 Old St Gregory's, Iż-Żejtun

Built in 1436, this simple whitewashed structure, topped with a shallow dome and bell tower, is one of the oldest surviving churches in Malta. ⚲ *Triq San Girgor • Map E5 • 2167 7187 • Open for Mass weekends • Festa first Wed after Easter*

7 Bir Miftuħ Chapel, Gudja

This graceful 15th-century church dedicated to St Mary of the Open Well now stands too close for comfort to the runways of Malta's international airport. Inside are the faded remnants of 17th-century murals. ⚲ *Gudja • Map E5 • 2122 0358 • Festa 15 Aug*

8 St George's Chapel, Birżebbuġa

Built by the Knights in 1683, this is the only fortified church on the coast. ⚲ *St George's Bay, Borġ In-Nadur • Map E6 • Mass in English 9:30am Sun*

9 St Mary, Il-Qrendi

Lorenzo Gafa transformed an older building into this handsome Baroque parish church in pretty Il-Qrendi. The rivalry between it and that of neighbouring L-Imqabba is legendary. ⚲ *Triq Il-Knisja • Map D6 • 2164 9395 • Festa 15 Aug*

10 Christ the King, Paola

Giuseppe D'Amato's modern church overlooks Paola's dreary suburban sprawl. D'Amato was also architect of the huge church in Ix-Xewkija, Gozo (see p39). ⚲ *Pjazza de Paule • Map E5 • 2169 5022*

Grabiel

Price Categories		
For a three course meal for one with half a bottle of wine (or equivalent meal), taxes and extra charges.	€	under €20
	€€	€20–€30
	€€€	€30–€40
	€€€€	€40–€50
	€€€€€	over €50

🔟 Restaurants and Cafés

1 Zonqor Point, Marsaskala

Specializing in Mediterranean cuisine, this friendly restaurant has been serving excellent fish for over 25 years. ⊗ *Triq Għar ix-Xama • Map F5 • 7970 4560 • Closed Mon L & D, Tue D (Wed D in winter) • €€*

2 Ir-Rizzu, Marsaxlokk

Fresh fish is the speciality at this great family-run restaurant overlooking the magnificent harbour. Book for Sunday lunch after the quayside fish market. ⊗ *52 Xatt Is-Sajjieda • Map F5 • 2165 1569 • Closed Sun D • €€*

3 Blue Creek Bar & Restaurant, Għar Lapsi

This smart, family-friendly spot looks out over the sea and the lido formed by a rocky inlet. It also has an inexpensive snack menu. ⊗ *Għar Lapsi • Map C6 • 2146 2800 • Closed Tue, Thu D • €€€*

4 Is-Sajjied Bar & Restaurant, Marsaxlokk

Another of Marsaxlokk's fine seafood restaurants, this has attractive nautical decor and a breezy terrace for summer dining. ⊗ *Xatt Is-Sajjieda • Map F5 • 2165 2549 • Closed Mon • €€*

5 Tal-Familja, Marsaskala

This spacious restaurant with rustic decor is great for local fish and Maltese cuisine. Daily specials are chalked up on a blackboard. ⊗ *Triq Il-Gardiel • Map F5 • 2163 2161 • Closed Mon • €€*

6 Pisces, Marsaxlokk

A long-standing stalwart of Marsaxlokk's dining scene, Pisces offers moderately priced seafood, along with Italian and Maltese fare. The glass-and-marble dining room is smarter than the slightly scruffy entrance suggests. ⊗ *89 Xatt Is-Sajjieda • Map F5 • 2165 4956 • Closed Sun–Tue D • €€*

7 La Favorita, Marsaskala

This friendly restaurant comes highly recommended by locals for its seafood specialities and relaxed atmosphere. It's on the edge of town, near St Thomas's Bay. Book at weekends. ⊗ *Triq Il-Gardiel • Map F5 • 2163 4113 • Closed Mon • €€*

8 Nargile Lounge, Marsaskala

An authentic Arab-style *shisha* lounge; enjoy Indian, Arabic and Mediterranean cuisine, speciality teas and a fruity hubble-bubble pipe. ⊗ *Triq Il-Gardiel • Map F5 • 2163 6734 • Closed L in summer • €*

9 Grabiel, Marsaskala

One of the islands' finest seafood restaurants – upmarket but not stuffy (see p57).

10 L-Ghenba Wine & Art, Iż-Żurrieq

Located in the southern part of the island, this restaurant is popular for wining and dining. It is easy on the pocket and also offers complimentary snacks. ⊗ *40, Misrah ir-Reppublika • Map D6 • €*

Left **The Citadel, Ir-Rabat/Victoria** Right **Calypso's Cave**

Around Gozo and Comino

OZO IS SMALLER, GREENER AND QUIETER *than its big sister, Malta. At its heart is the Citadel, the miniature central capital of this miniature island. From this tiny walled metropolis, beautiful views extend across the plains and out to sea. Nearby, the Ġgantija Temples are probably among the world's oldest freestanding monuments; gaze at these monumental ruins and ponder on the extraordinary culture that created them. The Gozitan coastline is breathtaking, particularly at Dwejra and the cliffs of Ta' Ċenċ, and the whole island is a walker's paradise. There's just one sandy beach, the ochre crescent of Ramla Bay, but countless coves and bays offer good spots for a dip. Smaller still, Comino is poised between Malta and Gozo; wild and largely empty, it boasts a population of four (or sometimes five). Droves of tourists descend daily to see the lovely Blue Lagoon, but in early morning and late afternoon the whole island returns to its habitual slumber.*

🏆10 Sights

1. The Citadel, Ir-Rabat/ Victoria
2. Ġgantija Temples
3. Dwejra
4. Santa Marija Bay, Comino
5. Blue Lagoon, Comino
6. Xewkija Rotunda
7. Ramla Bay
8. Calypso's Cave, Ramla Bay
9. Ta' Ċenċ Cliffs
10. Ta' Pinu Basilica, L-Għarb

Dwejra

For a good overview of Gozo's history, check out the Gozo 360° audiovisual show at the Citadel Theatre in Ir-Rabat/Victoria.

Ġgantija Temples

The Citadel, Ir-Rabat/ Victoria

At the physical and spiritual heart of Gozo, this tiny walled city sits high on a rocky bluff, commanding views of virtually the whole island. A citadel has existed here since Roman times, but the current structure was built in the 17th century after the previous walls were breached by the corsair Dragut Rais. Gozitans still refer to their capital as Ir-Rabat, even though it was officially renamed Victoria to celebrate the British Queen's Diamond Jubilee in 1897 *(see pp24–5)*.

Ġgantija Temples

The huge, pale stones of Ġgantija have stood for more than five and a half millennia – over a thousand years longer than the pyramids of Egypt.

Despite its age, this temple complex is one of the best-preserved in the Maltese archipelago, with sturdy walls reaching up to 7 m (23 ft) in height *(see p35)*.

Dwejra

Dwejra's sheer cliffs, curving bays, gigantic caves and entrancing rock formations combine to make it Gozo's most celebrated photo opportunity. Although tourists gather in droves at the foot of the striking Azure Window (a rocky opening framing stunning views), it's possible to strike out along the cliff paths to enjoy the panorama in relative peace *(see pp26–7)*.

Santa Marija Bay, Comino

There are two attractive bays, both with sought-after strips of sand, on the island of Comino, but this one is public while the other is private. Out of season you may well find you have it all to yourself *(see p47)*.

Blue Lagoon, Comino

The main draw on Comino is the magical Blue Lagoon, the focus of innumerable daily boat cruises. Those staying on the island can enjoy it without the hordes of day-trippers *(see p47)*.

Blue Lagoon, Comino

The Xagħra Circle

An underground burial chamber similar to the famous Ħal Saflieni Hypogeum *(see pp22–3)* is being excavated near the Ġgantija Temples. The early excavation notes for the Hypogeum were lost, so the careful exploration of the Xagħra Circle has enormous importance for archaeologists seeking to understand the world of the Maltese temple-builders. This site was neither as large nor as lavishly decorated as Ħal Saflieni, but the ongoing excavation works have advanced understanding of prehistoric burial rites to a remarkable degree.

6 Xewkija Rotunda

Just as the Mosta Dome dominates much of the island of Malta, so the Xewkija Rotunda is visible from almost everywhere in Gozo. It is Europe's third-largest dome, although the people of Il-Mosta claim theirs is bigger. Architect Giuseppe D'Amato was inspired by the Basilica of Santa Maria Della Salute in Venice. His church is made of local limestone. It was begun in 1951 and took 20 years to build *(see p39)*.

7 Ramla Bay

Ramla has Gozo's best beach, backed by gentle hills with tumbling terraces. It's also the only truly sandy beach on the island. Out of season, it feels like a corner of paradise, but at the height of the summer it can get unbearably crowded. Almost 2,000 years ago, a Roman villa was built on this idyllic spot. You can see the sparse remains close to the beach *(see p47)*.

8 Calypso's Cave, Ramla Bay

In this lofty cave, carved out of the rock high above Ramla Bay, the love-sick nymph Calypso is said to have seduced Odysseus in Homer's epic *The Odyssey*. Get there by scrambling up the short but steep path which leads from the beachfront. (Ask in the café for directions.) Once at the entrance, you can stroll through the pretty manicured little garden to the lookout point to enjoy tremendous views. Steps lead down to the cave itself, which is disappointingly dank and rubbish-filled. If you do scramble all the way down, the rocks open onto the sea, framing more stunning views. Gazing out at the endless, cobalt sea, it's easy to imagine the nymph whispering sweet nothings to her reluctant lover.

§ *Follow signs from Ix-Xagħra • Map E1 • Open 9am–dusk • Free*

9 Ta' Ċenċ Cliffs

This stretch of wild cliffs, which plunge sheerly and terrifyingly into the sea below, is one of the most beautiful sights in Gozo. Go at dusk, when the cliffs are flushed pink by the setting sun. For centuries, bird-trappers swung down these cliffs in rough slings on ropes. Hunting and trapping are now banned, but few Maltese hunters

Ramla Bay

Get off the beaten track in the southeastern corner of Gozo, beyond Il-Qala, where there's some fine hiking and quiet coves.

Ta' Ċenċ Cliffs

seem to have taken note, and the local bird population has suffered terribly as a result. Nonetheless, numerous bird species continue to make the Ta' Ċenċ cliffs their home *(see p42)*.

Ta' Pinu Basilica, L-Għarb
10 The Ta' Pinu Basilica is Gozo's most important place of pilgrimage. Our Lady of Ta' Pinu is credited with miraculous healing powers, and numerous ex-votos (including crutches and artificial limbs) attest to prayers being answered. The huge modern church (which was completed in 1931) retains a section of the original 19th-century chapel where, in 1883, a local woman is reputed to have seen a vision of Our Lady *(see p39)*.

Ta' Pinu Basilica, L-Għarb

A Tour around Gozo

Morning

Set off early, so that you can arrive at the cliffs of **Dwejra** *(see pp26–7)* in time to enjoy them without the crowds. Take a boat ride from the **Inland Sea** through to the **Azure Window**. Take some time to stroll along the cliff paths and enjoy spectacular views of **Fungus Rock** and the rugged coastline. Drive to **Victoria** (which locals still call Ir-Rabat) to explore the lofty walled **citadel** *(see pp24–5)*. Don't miss the frothy Baroque **cathedral** and the excellent **Museum of Archaeology**. You can have a simple but delicious lunch of fresh bread and local cheese at Ta' Rikardu *(see p103)*.

Afternoon

After lunch, drive to nearby **Ix-Xagħra** to see the ancient **Ġgantija Temples**, in a beautiful setting overlooking a wide, green plain. The same ticket also gains admission to the **Ta' Kola Windmill** on the outskirts of the village. Head next to the village square, where one of the little café-bars should be open for a drink. If you have enough time, you could drive on for another 10 minutes to **Ramla Bay**, Gozo's best beach, for a refreshing dip. Then return to the other side of the island and make for Ta' Sannat, following the signs for **Ta' Ċenċ**. Spend an enjoyable hour strolling around these magnificent cliffs as dusk falls. Finally, you could dine on fresh fish at Sammy's *(see p103)*, on the waterfront in **Mġarr Harbour**, finishing the day with a drink at the nearby Gleneagles Bar, which has a fantastic terrace overlooking the port.

Left **Mġarr harbour, L-Imġarr** Right **St George's Basilica**

Best of the Rest

1 Folklore Museum, L-Għarb
An engaging little museum in one of Gozo's prettiest, least spoilt villages. It has a collection of tools, costumes, paintings and curiosities typical of rural Gozitan life. ◈ *99 Church Square • Map D1 • 2156 1929 • Open 9am–4pm Mon–Sat, 9am–1pm Sun • Adm charge*

2 St George's Basilica, Ir-Rabat/Victoria
Known as the "Golden Church" for its dazzling, gilded interior, this sumptuous Baroque edifice was designed by Vittorio Cassar and completed in 1673. Inside is a curious statue of St George carved from a single tree. ◈ *Pjazza San Ġorġ • Map D2 • 2155 6377 • Open for Mass daily • Free*

3 Ta' Kola Windmill, Ix-Xagħra
Built in 1725, this is the only survivor of twelve windmills built by the Knights. All kinds of objects related to traditional Maltese crafts are gathered here in an interesting little museum. ◈ *Triq Maija Bambina • Map E1 • 2156 1071 • Open 9am–5:15pm daily • Adm charge • www.heritagemalta.org*

4 Ta' Dbieġi Crafts Village, L-Għarb
Gozo's craft village is not as big as Malta's but is still convenient for souvenir shopping. There are demonstrations of traditional crafts, and it's a good place to pick up Gozitan woollen jumpers and rugs. ◈ *Triq San Lawrenz • Map D1 • Open 9:30am–5pm Mon–Sat*

5 Xlendi Bay
This once-beautiful bay, between silvery cliffs, has been spoilt by careless development, but it remains one of Gozo's most popular resorts *(see p47)*.

6 Marsalforn
Once a tiny fishing village, Marsalforn is now a sprawling, but still low-key, resort on Gozo's northern coast *(see p47)*.

7 Salt Pans, Reqqa Point
Hundreds of salt pans indent the soft limestone near Marsalforn, forming a surreal landscape of strange, natural beauty *(see p42)*.

8 San Blas Bay
This beautiful little bay, with its strip of ochre sand, is hard to reach (you'll need to scramble down a steep footpath), but it's well worth it *(see p42)*.

9 Mġarr Harbour, L-Imġarr
Guarded by a fortress and hemmed in by cliffs, the focus of the village is still the salty old port, full of colourful *luzzus* and vivid blue fishing nets. ◈ *Map F2*

10 Comino Tower (St Mary's Tower), Comino
It wasn't until 1618 that Comino got long-promised fortifications to protect it from pirates. This tower still guards the island's southwestern approaches, and has been restored to its former glory. ◈ *Map F3*

A combination of local bread, Gozitan cheese, fresh tomatoes and some local wine make a great picnic.

Price Categories

For a three-course meal for one with half a bottle of wine (or equivalent meal), taxes and extra charges.

€	under €20
€€	€20–€30
€€€	€30–€40
€€€€	€40–€50
€€€€€	over €50

Zeppi's Pub

🔟 Restaurants and Cafés

1 Waterbiscuit, St Julian's

Enjoy indoor or outdoor dining at this eatery serving innovative, contemporary cuisine (see p57).

2 Il-Kċina Tal-Barrakka (Sammy's), Mġarr Harbour

This harbourside eaterie is one of the best places to try fresh fish. It's run by the same owners as the fabulous Gleneagles Bar nearby. Book well in advance. ◈ 28 Manoel de Vilhena Street, L-Imġarr • Map F2 • 9921 3801 • Closed Nov–Apr; May–Oct: Thu–Tue L, Sun D • €€€

3 Ta' Frenc, Gozo

This exceptional restaurant, serving excellent Maltese and Mediterranean dishes in a stylishly restored old farmhouse, is often considered the best in all Malta (see p56).

4 Il-Kartell, Marsalforn

This well-established favourite of locals and tourists alike is situated at the water's edge. It offers a wide Maltese and Mediterranean menu. ◈ Marsalforn Marina • Map E1 • 2155 6918 • €€

5 Patrick's Tmun, Ir-Rabat/ Victoria

An elegant restaurant decorated with contemporary art, this is popular with a well-heeled local crowd. Go for the six-course "tasting menu". ◈ Triq Europe • Map D2 • 2156 6667 • Closed Mon–Sat L, Sun D in winter • €€€

6 Jeffrey's, L-Għarb

A perennial favourite, this rustically furnished village restaurant serves up delicious and authentic local cuisine at bargain prices (see p56).

7 Ta' Rikardu, Ir-Rabat/ Victoria

Conveniently located right next to the cathedral in the Citadel, this rustic little spot serves delicious local bread, cheese and wine (see p56).

8 Dvenue, Ix-Xagħra

This establishment blends Gozitan taste with modern chic. The menu includes freshly home-made pasta, fish dishes and traditional specialities such as rabbit and local lamb. ◈ 32 Victory Square • Map E1 • 2156 6542 • €€

9 Comino Hotel, Comino

It's best to bring a picnic and find your own quiet corner if you want to avoid the crowds on Comino. This hotel has the only restaurant on the island, offering reasonable Mediterranean cuisine. ◈ San Niklaw Bay • Map F2 • 2152 9821 • Closed Nov–Feb • €€€

10 Zeppi's Pub, Il-Qala

This attractive village pub offers a great range of imaginative lunchtime snacks, including salads, omelettes and croques monsieurs. The art gallery upstairs also sells wonderful gifts. ◈ St Joseph Square • Map F2 • 9924 2138 • Closed Mon L • €

STREETSMART

MALTA'S TOP 10

Left **Luqa Airport** Right **A bus below L'Imdina town**

📖 Getting to and Around Malta

1 By Air
Malta International Airport is at Ħal Luqa, about 8 km (5 miles) from Valletta. The national airline Air Malta connects with more than 50 major cities. A few other big carriers, including Alitalia, Lufthansa and Emirates, also fly to Ħal Luqa, as well as budget airlines Ryanair and easyJet. ◈ Map D5 • 2124 9600 • www.maltairport.com

2 Charters and Packages
Many charter flights and flight/hotel packages are available – especially in the summer season, but deals are available year-round. Flight-only deals are hard to come by in July and August.

3 Cruises
Valletta is a stopover on many Mediterranean cruises, with a modern terminal right on the beautiful Grand Harbour. The approach to Valletta by ship is unforgettable: the view has barely changed in five centuries. Smaller ships may dock at Xlendi Harbour, Gozo.

4 Sailing
Malta's spectacular harbours and quaint coves have attracted sailors for thousands of years. The two biggest marinas are in Marsamxett Harbour, between Valletta and Tas-Sliema. The Maritime Authority, Customs Office and Royal Malta Yacht Club are all nearby. Pleasure craft may anchor for the night in all bays and inlets except at Filfla Island. ◈ Transport Malta-Ports and Yachting Directorate, Marsa • 2122 2203

5 Getting Around by Bus
Malta's picturesque, much-photographed old snub-nosed buses have now been replaced, but the new services can be unreliable due to a shortage of drivers. Nevertheless this is a cheap way of getting around, and the routes are fairly comprehensive. Most services on Malta begin at Valletta, while on Gozo, Ir-Rabat/Victoria is the main terminus. ◈ Valletta bus terminal, City Gate • Gozo bus terminal, Main City Gate, Ir-Rabat/Victoria

6 Sightseeing by Bus
Another excellent way to get around Malta and Gozo is by hop-on-hop-off bus. These operate on four routes, taking in all the major sights and landmarks. There is a shuttle that picks up and drops off at hotels, and a "Malta by Night" tour.

7 Getting Around by Ferry
Gozo Channel Company operates a car and passenger ferry between Ċirkewwa (Malta) and Mġarr Harbour (Gozo). A passenger-only ferry links Tas-Sliema and Valletta. The Comino Hotel runs a small ferry to Comino, but local boat tours make regular runs to the Blue Lagoon from Mġarr Harbour and Ċirkewwa.

8 Getting Around: Boat Excursions
One of the most enjoyable ways to see the Maltese islands is by boat. Some of the prettiest coves and most dramatic stretches of coastline can only be reached by sea. Tour operators are based in Tas-Sliema or Xlendi (Gozo).

9 Getting Around by Car
A car is invaluable to get off the beaten track. But be prepared for pot-holed roads, decrepit vehicles and Maltese drivers' blithe disregard for speed limits and other road-users. All major rental firms are at the airport; local firms are cheaper and usually very reliable.

10 Getting Around on Foot
Despite the development that has mushroomed across the islands, Malta still has a few unspoilt corners with spellbinding scenery. Hiking is popular and best in spring, when flowers carpet the fields and the islands are cooler and quieter. There are several good walking guides; check them out at Agenda Bookshop (see p64).

Left **Dual-language street sign** Right **Tourist Information Office**

TOP 10 General Information

1 Climate
Malta has a typically Mediterranean climate: hot, sunny summers, mild winters, and low rainfall. In spring and autumn the islands can be affected by the *sirocco*, a scorching wind from Africa. The bitingly cold *gregale* brings storms. July and August are the hottest months, September and October the wettest.

2 When to Go
Malta's high season runs from late June to September. If you can, avoid the crowds and heat of July and August; in September and June the islands are warm but less crowded. Spring is beautiful, before the intense greens and vivid wild flowers give way to dusty browns and greys.

3 Passports and Visas
Malta joined the EU in 2004 (so EU residents have no travel restrictions) and the Schengen zone in 2008 (so anyone with a valid Schengen visa can enter the country). Depending on your nationality, a visa is needed for stays for longer than 90 days; check the Maltese Foreign Affairs website. ⊗ *www.foreign.gov.mt*

4 Embassies and Consulates
Maltese embassies and consulates can supply information about visiting, studying, working, or retiring in Malta. The Maltese foreign ministry website *(see above)* has a directory of offices.

5 Tourist Offices Abroad
The helpful Malta Tourism Authority (MTA) is a useful first port of call when planning your trip. It has offices in Australia and many European countries including the UK. Addresses are listed on its website. ⊗ *www.visitmalta.com*

6 Tourist Offices in Malta
Malta's main tourist information office is in Valletta, on Merchants Street (map reference H3). The friendly staff can provide information on everything from bus routes to local *festas*. There is also an office in Ir-Rabat/Victoria (Gozo), and a booth at the airport.

7 Internet Information
The official tourist website, *www.visitmalta.com*, has comprehensive information on everything to see and do, and a useful interactive map. For information on *festas* and other events, check out *www.maltafestivals.com*. For affectionate insights into the islands, try *www.my-malta.com*. The website *www.gozo.com* provides a wealth of information on Gozo. The leading newspaper, *The Times of Malta*, has an informative website: *www.timesofmalta.com*.

8 Language
Maltese and English are the official languages. Maltese is closely related to Arabic, but uses the Latin alphabet with a few special marks *(see p126)*. You'll hear it spoken everywhere, but virtually everyone can speak English. Almost all of the street signs are in Maltese, but most shops and businesses use the English version in advertising. All road signs are in English.

9 Time Differences
Malta keeps Central European Time (CET), an hour ahead of GMT, but (as elsewhere in Europe) the clocks go forward one hour in summer. It is one hour ahead of the UK, six hours ahead of New York and nine hours ahead of California.

10 Local Customs
The Maltese are devout Catholics. Dress suitably when entering a church (no shorts or strappy tops), and behave respectfully – or expect to be admonished by a tutting usher. Topless sunbathing is prohibited on public beaches, but tolerated on private ones. Unofficial car park attendants expect a tip (€1 average) but it's not compulsory.

Left **Village police station** Right **Valletta pharmacy**

Security and Health

Emergency Numbers

In an emergency, dial 112 for the police, fire brigade or ambulance. To report a traffic accident that doesn't need emergency services, call local wardens on 2132 0202. For non-urgent matters, contact police head-quarters (see below).

Police

Every town and village has its own police station, easily spotted by the blue lantern outside in traditional British style. National police wear blue uniforms and should be contacted to report a crime. Police headquarters are in Floriana (Malta) and Ir-Rabat/Victoria (Gozo). Green-uniformed traffic wardens are responsible for road safety. Pjazza Vicenzo Buġeja, Floriana • 2294 0000 • Triq Ir-Repubblika, Ir-Rabat/Victoria • 2156 2040

Health Issues

By far the most common health problems for holiday-makers are caused by excessive sun. Always use sunscreen, drink plenty of water, and wear a hat in the open. Take particular care with small children. The water is safe to drink but tastes unpleasant. Bottled water is widely available.

Prescriptions

Most well-known medicines are easy to get in Malta. If you may need a repeat prescription, it's best to bring a doctor's letter to avoid problems with customs or the pharmacist. Note the generic name, as well as the brand name, of any drugs you may need.

Pharmacies

Every town and village has one or more chemists, identified by a green cross sign. Most follow normal shop hours, closing for lunch. Check the local papers to find out which ones are open on Sunday. Pharmacists can usually advise on simple health problems.

Disabled Travellers

The Maltese islands are not ideally equipped for disabled travellers, although things are very slowly improving. Hotels and restaurants in older buildings have virtually no facilities for wheelchair-users, although the accommodating Maltese will usually try their best to help. All new hotels, restaurants and visitors' attractions provide good disabled facilities. Buses do not generally have wheelchair access.

Women Travellers

Women visitors will have no difficulties in Malta, where the locals are friendly, open and generous. Drunken tourists can be more annoying. There's very little violent crime and no real "no-go" areas. But be aware that the culture is deeply traditional and the Catholic Church still exerts a huge influence – divorce and abortion, for example, are still illegal.

Gay Travellers

Malta decriminalized homosexuality in 1973. Although it remains a traditional society, gay travellers are welcomed with typical Maltese generosity, and there is a well-established, if small, gay scene. Regular club nights are organized and more new places are opening. As for beaches, Ġnejna Bay and Fomm Ir-Rih Bay (see p82) are gay-friendly. www.gaymalta.org

Insurance

All visitors are recommended to take out travel insurance. EU citizens should note that reciprocal agreements don't cover, for example, dentistry and repatriation, and the bureaucracy can be hard to untangle.

Crime

There is comparatively little crime in Malta. Watch out for bag-snatchers or pickpockets in crowded resorts or at the beach, and try to keep your bag strapped across you. Avoid leaving anything in an unattended car, and leave the glove compartment open to show that it is empty. Report any crime to the police immediately.

Left **Valletta post box** Centre **Valletta telephone box** Right **International newspaper**

TOP10 Banking and Communications

Currency
1 Malta has used the euro since January 2008, when it replaced the Maltese lira. Euro coins come in 1, 2, 5, 10, 20 and 50 euro cents, and €1 and €2. Notes come in denominations of €5, €10, €20, €50, €100, €200 and €500.

Changing Money
2 Cash and traveller's cheques can be readily exchanged at banks, bureaux de change and most hotels (although hotels often offer poor rates and charge high commissions). Banks usually offer the best rates and can be found in all the larger towns and resorts. It may be cheapest to use a debit card to withdraw money from an ATM machine.

Banking Hours
3 Banks' opening hours are usually 8:30am–1:30pm Mon–Thu, 8:30am–3:30pm Fri and 8:30am–12:30pm on Sat. Some banks in larger towns and resorts may open one or two afternoons a week, but those in smaller towns often close on Saturday mornings in summer.

Cash Dispensers
4 There are plenty of cash machines (ATMs) throughout the islands, at least in the larger towns and resorts. Look for an illuminated sign bearing a bank logo. They accept major debit and credit cards 24 hours a day. Instructions are available in English, French, German, Italian and Maltese.

Credit Cards
5 Credit cards are accepted at most moderate to expensive hotels and restaurants, and at most shops. But few budget hotels, small guesthouses and shops, or cheaper cafés and restaurants take them; nor do many museums. Mastercard and Visa are the most widely accepted, American Express and Diners Club less so.

Post
6 The Maltese postal system is generally reliable. Most larger towns have post offices, which are usually open 7:30am–12:45pm Mon–Sat. Main branches, such as those in Valletta and Ir-Rabat/Victoria (Gozo), stay open until 4:30pm and are also open on Saturday mornings. Post boxes are bright red, an appealing British tradition.

Telephones
7 Telephone boxes – also often in British-style scarlet, but otherwise green or clear – are easy to find in most towns and resorts. Most use phone cards (called Telecards and available from newsagents for €5, €10 and €20. In many old-fashioned bars and cafés it's acceptable to use the phone for local calls, leaving usually 50c.

Internet Cafés
8 All larger towns and resorts have Internet cafés. They seem to pop up and disappear without warning, so check with a tourist office or try the local website *(see below)* for a list. Some phone boxes give Internet access. ✆ *www.internetcafe.com.mt*

Newspapers and Magazines
9 Malta's leading newspaper is *The Times*, which famously continued to publish every day of World War II. *The Independent* has a similar conservative stance but a lower circulation. *Malta Today* is published twice weekly. All three are English-language. *In-Nazzjon* and *L-Orizzont* are the main Maltese-language papers. British and other European publications are usually available the day after publication. ✆ *www.timesofmalta.com*

Television
10 There are three main local TV stations. One is publicly owned, another is owned by the Labour Party and the third by the Nationalist Party. There's also good reception of Italian channels. Cable and satellite are hugely popular. Most hotels, even the most modest, have satellite television.

Left **Silversmith making filigree jewellery** Centre **Street market** Right **Self-catering apartment**

TOP 10 Eating, Shopping and Lodging

1 Restaurant Guide

The annually updated *Definitive(ly) Good Guide to Restaurants* is a pocket-sized gourmet bible for many island residents, reflecting the opinions of restaurant-goers rather than critics. It is available from local bookshops, and you can recoup the cost by using discount vouchers at the back. The maps are also very useful.

2 When to Eat

The Maltese tend to eat their main meal at lunchtime, and they like to eat a lot; there are often five or six courses, and lunch may last for several hours, especially at weekends. Eating times are similar to those of northern Europe: lunch about 1pm and dinner about 8pm.

3 Restaurant Opening Hours

Most restaurants in major resorts open for lunch and dinner in the high season, but have reduced hours (or even close altogether) in winter. Valletta is different: it virtually shuts down in the evening, and some restaurants are open for lunch only. Restaurants in the country and smaller villages are also likely to close in the evenings.

4 Self-catering and Picnicking

There is plenty of self-catering accommodation in Malta, from budget apartments in resorts to beautifully restored Gozitan farmhouses and historic apartments in Valletta. The best food is often the simplest – heavenly bread, plump tomatoes and peppered Gozitan cheese that are perfect for picnics.

5 What to Buy

Malta has long been known for its jewellery, particularly silver filigree. Maltese crosses are also popular buys. Woollen jumpers and rugs from Gozo are expensive but make great souvenirs. The islands are also famous for lace, but most of what you'll see is machine-made. Handmade lace is harder to find and more expensive, but beautiful. Colourful hand-blown glass from L-Imdina and local ceramics also make attractive souvenirs.

6 Maltese Craft Villages

Malta and Gozo both have craft villages *(see pp88, 102)*, where you'll find all the traditional local crafts and can buy souvenirs at reasonable prices. Both craft villages also give demonstrations.

7 Shopping Hours

Smaller shops usually open from 9am to 1 or 2pm and from 3 or 4pm to about 7pm. Many close for a half-day once a week, and many also on Saturday afternoons. Department stores, chain stores and bigger shops stay open at midday, and those in big towns (such as Tas-Sliema) often until 8 or 9pm. Virtually nothing is open on Sundays, except in resort areas.

8 Markets

Valletta has a daily market for clothes, CDs, souvenirs, etc, and a big Sunday flea market. On the quays at Marsaxlokk there's a tourist market, with a colourful and pungent fish market on Sundays. For the freshest fruit and vegetables, buy from produce vans to be found parked on corners.

9 Low-season Bargains

April and October are usually cheaper than July to September, but for the best bargains visit Malta in winter. Accommodation prices plummet, and fantastic bargains can be had by shopping around.

10 Websites for Hotel Discounts

Tour operators block-book many hotels, and may be cheapest overall. The tourism authority doesn't offer a hotel-booking service, but its website has a hotel-search facility. Several websites offer discounts on Maltese hotels – but double-check with the hotel's own website to make sure it isn't offering even better deals.

⊕ www.visitmalta.com

• www.hotelclub.net

 Some of Valletta's restaurants don't open in the evenings; call in advance.

Left **Unattended valuables** Centre **Sunbathers** Right **Parking in Valletta**

TOP 10 Things to Avoid

1 Hunters

Malta has more than 16,000 hunters and trappers in a population of under 400,000. They kill 2–3 million birds a year, including endangered species protected under European and Maltese law. Gun-toting hunters regularly haunt some of the most beautiful and unspoilt corners (ignoring hunting seasons and protected areas), so be wary while out hiking. Contact the conservation group BirdLife Malta for more information.
❧ www.birdlifemalta.org

2 Driving

Malta has the highest road-accident rate in Europe. It's best to avoid driving altogether – especially in Valletta, where it can be extremely difficult to park – but if you do get behind the wheel, remember that Maltese drivers don't believe in speed restrictions, using indicators or giving way. Expect any courtesy you show to be treated as a sign of weakness. Be especially wary of buses; their drivers treat other road-users as invisible.

3 Visiting in August

Malta's population explodes in August, when nearly 200,000 visitors arrive. Rooms are scarce and expensive, beaches are crammed, and the heat excessive. On the plus side, the beach-holiday requisites of sun, sea and sand are all at their peak and it's a good season for *festas*.

4 Leaving Valuables in a Car

Malta has less crime than most other parts of Europe, but thieves have begun to target cars parked in rural areas. So take all valuables with you and open the glove compartment to show there is nothing of value.

5 Sleeping in Paċeville

Paċeville is Malta's party capital, with dozens of bars crammed in a few small streets. It's popular with teenagers, who hang out on the streets until the small hours. The hotels in the area are best left to night owls.

6 Relying on Opening Times

In Malta, as in much of the Mediterranean, time is a fluid concept. Don't expect posted opening hours in museums, shops or restaurants to be exact. Everything may close without notice – or stay open later than you expect. If you are particularly keen to see a museum or eat at a certain restaurant, it's wise to phone ahead.

7 Excessive Sun

Northern European visitors are easy to spot in Malta: they are usually shiny and scarlet. The Maltese themselves are avid, but sensible, sun-worshippers. Follow their example and avoid sun-bathing between noon and 4pm, always use a good sunscreen, and drink plenty of water.

8 Smoking

Smoking is banned in all public places, including restaurants, bars, shops, public areas in hotels, and the airport. Many restaurants and bars have outdoor smoking areas, and a few larger establishments have smoking sections.

9 Wasting Water

Water is scarce. Try to save it by taking showers rather than baths, turning the tap off while brushing teeth or shaving, and asking your hotel to change sheets and towels less often.

10 Unscrupulous Taxi Drivers

Some taxi drivers try to charge whatever they think passengers will pay, rather than the official rates posted near taxi ranks. Taxis should use their meters, but almost never do, so agree the fare in advance. There are no supplements for luggage, for extra passengers (up to four), or for the day or time of the journey. Contact the Malta Transport Authority with complaints. ❧ *Sa Maison Road, Floriana • 2560 8000 • www. maltatransport.com*

Left **Hilton Malta, St Julian's** Centre **Hotel Phoenicia Malta, Floriana** Right **Ta' Ċenċ, Ta' Sannat (Gozo)**

🔟 Luxury Retreats

1 Corinthia Hotel, St George's Bay
A private beach and beautiful views of the sea enhance the experience of staying at this family-friendly resort. The rooms are spacious and there is a separate club for kids. It also has several restaurants and swimming pools. Free access to Wi-Fi is available. ◊ *St Julian's • Map C4 • 2137 4114 • €€€ • www.corinthia.com*

2 The Palace Malta, Tas-Sliema
Located close to Tas-Sliema's shops, cafés and bars, this excellent hotel is equipped with comfortable and stylish rooms. Amenities include a spa, fitness room and an indoor and outdoor swimming pool. The restaurant, Temptasian, on the top floor offers superb views of Valletta. Friendly staff. ◊ *High Street • Map Q3 • 2133 3444 • €€€ • www.thepalacemalta.com*

3 Radisson Blu Resort and Spa, Malta Golden Sands, Golden Bay
Huge and glossy, this resort hotel overlooks one of Malta's best beaches and offers every five-star luxury. It has extensive sports facilities, a large spa, and a private sandy beach. It is also secluded, the only hotel in the bay. ◊ *Map A3 • 2356 1000 • €€€€€ • www.radissonsas.com*

4 Fortina Spa Resort, Tas-Sliema
Enjoy your own en-suite spa – plus, in some rooms, a private roof terrace and sea-water pool, and/or a view of Valletta. This vast complex includes fitness and diving centres, and eight restaurants. ◊ *Tigne Seafront • Map R3 • 2346 0000 • €€€ • www.hotelfortina.com*

5 Hotel Phoenicia Malta, Floriana
Formal afternoon tea is still served at this 1920s *grande dame*. The hotel is set in seven acres of landscaped gardens just outside Valletta's city walls, and many rooms enjoy wonderful harbour views. There's an outdoor pool. ◊ *The Mall • Map G3 • 2122 5241 • €€€€ • www.phoeniciamalta.com*

6 Radisson SAS Bay Point Resort, St Julian's
This vast resort hotel has it all: elegant boutiques, diving and water-sports centres, business facilities and a whole range of restaurants and bars. ◊ *St George's Bay • Map D3 • 2137 4894 • €€€€ • www.radissonsas.com*

7 Hilton Malta, St Julian's
Part of the development beside Spinola Bay, the Hilton offers every luxury, from a private beach club to its own marina. There are pools, a gym, a dance studio, tennis and squash courts, and various health and beauty treatments. ◊ *Portomaso • Map P1 • 2138 3383 • €€€€€ • www.hilton.com*

8 Le Méridien St Julian's
This stylish hotel is set in a 19th-century villa overlooking Balluta Bay. Amenities include the spectacular Lotus Spa in a glass atrium and several restaurants under an award-winning chef. ◊ *39 Triq Il-Kbira, Balluta Bay • Map P2 • 2311 0000 • €€€€ • www.malta.lemeridien.com*

9 Ta' Ċenċ, Sannat, Gozo
The romantic, village-style Ta' Ċenċ's rooms and apartments are built from creamy limestone; the circular "trullos" are most desirable. There's a spa, gardens, pools, gym and outdoor restaurant. A shuttle bus serves a private lido. ◊ *Map E2 • 2155 6819 • €€€€ • www.vjborg.com/tacenc*

10 Kempinski St Lawrenz Resort & Spa, Gozo
Built of creamy stone and set in subtropical gardens, this is a stylish and tranquil retreat. It is one of Europe's finest spas, and offers Ayurveda and other different but complementary health and beauty treatments. ◊ *Triq Ir-Rokon • Map D1 • 2211 0000 • €€€€ • www.kempinski-gozo.com*

 The standard of accommodation in Malta has improved dramatically over the last few years, with many new luxury hotels.

Dar Ta' Zeppi

Characterful Places to Stay

1 Hotel Juliani, St Julian's

Malta's first boutique hotel is still the epitome of urban cool, furnished in a slick mix of antique and contemporary. Its restaurants and bars are the most fashionable on buzzy Spinola Bay. The tiny rooftop pool and deck offer fabulous views. ⊗ *25 Triq San Ġorġ • Map N1 • 2138 8000 • €€€ • www.hoteljuliani.com*

2 Xara Palace, Hotel L-Imdina

Housed within a magnificent palace within the walls of the "Silent City", this is the perfect spot to soak up L-Imdina's atmosphere when the tour groups have left. Its restaurants, particularly De Mondion (*see p89*), are superb, and it has a luxurious spa. ⊗ *Misraħ Il-Kunsill • Map C4 • 2145 0560 • €€€€€ • www.xarapalace.com.mt*

3 Hotel Castille, Valletta

A welcoming hotel in a rosy-pink Baroque palace. There's a great rooftop restaurant with views to the Grand Harbour and a cosy, vaulted pizza restaurant in the cellar. ⊗ *Misraħ Kastilja • Map H3 • 2124 3677 • € • www.hotelcastillemalta.com*

4 Corinthia Palace Hotel and Spa, Attard

Birthplace of the international Corinthia brand, this five-star hotel offers excellent facilities such as a large swimming pool, a spa and many good restaurants. The Mediterranean gardens add to its appeal. ⊗ *De Paule Avenue • Map C4 • 2144 0301 • €€€ • www.corinthia.com*

5 Valletta G-House, Valletta

An unusual, charming and romantic apartment in a beautiful historic building. It is stylishly decorated with *objets d'art*, paintings and antiques, but has 21st-century gadgets. Guests are met at the airport, and a welcome basket awaits. ⊗ *Triq Il-Fran • Map J2 • 781 39 888 27 • €€€€€ • www.vallettahouse.com*

6 Imperial Hotel, Tas-Sliema

The Imperial retains 19th-century details, including a sweeping staircase that once featured in a James Bond movie. The lobby has a glittering chandelier and glossy marble, but the rooms are rather bland. There's a garden with stone arches and a large outdoor pool. ⊗ *Triq Rodolfu • Map P2 • 2134 4094 • € • www.imperialhotelmalta.com*

7 Maritim Antoine Hotel & Spa, Il-Mellieħa

This peach-painted hotel has a commanding view, and is one of the most attractive in Il-Mellieħa. One pool is set in lush gardens, another on the roof, and a third indoors. ⊗ *Triq Borġ Olivier • Map B2 • 2289 2000 • €€ • www.maritim.com.mt*

8 Mia Casa Bed & Breakfast, Victoria/Rabat, Gozo

The hospitality of hosts Kevin and Jo creates a warm and homely atmosphere at this centrally-located bed and breakfast place. The food served here is delicious. ⊗ *23 Triq Santa Marija • Map D1 • 2730 0169 • €*

9 Dar Ta' Zeppi, Il-Qala, Gozo

There are just two stylish, high-ceilinged rooms in this beautiful house, each big enough for a family. Tanja, a superb cook, prepares spectacular Mediterranean cuisine in the evenings, while Victor regales guests with stories. There's a lovely pool in the garden. ⊗ *39 28th April 1688 Street • Map F2 • 2155 5051 • € • www.dartazeppi.com*

10 Xagħra Lodge, Ix-Xagħra, Gozo

A British couple run this cosy guesthouse, with quintessentially English decor, in a sleepy village. It has a honeymoon suite with four-poster bed, family rooms and a pool in the garden. ⊗ *Triq Dun George Preca • Map E1 • 2156 2362 • € • www.xagħralodge.com*

Left **Gillieru Harbour** Right **Comino Hotel**

TOP 10 Seaside Charmers

1 Comino Hotel, Comino

The only accommodation on Comino, this pink-painted hotel overlooks a little bay and private beach, so you can enjoy the island's peace once the day-trippers have left. The rooms are simple, but there are good sports facilities. Prices are for half-board. ⚲ *San Niklaw Bay • Map F2 • 2152 9821 • Open Apr–Oct • €€ • www.cominohotel.com*

2 Grand Hotel, L-Imġarr, Gozo

From its commanding position on the hill above Mġarr Harbour, the Grand gives magnificent views of the port and its brightly painted fishing boats. The prettiest rooms have private balconies that overlook the port. The restaurant is one of the best on Gozo, and has a breezy summer terrace. ⚲ *Triq Sant' Anton, Għajnsielem • Map E2 • 2156 3840 • €€ • www.grandhotelmalta.com*

3 St Patrick's Hotel, Ix-Xlendi, Gozo

A smart, whitewashed hotel right by the sea. The rooms have rather dated furnishings but the best have a Jacuzzi and a terrace overlooking the magnificent bay. There's a small rooftop pool with sun deck and a popular seafront restaurant. ⚲ *Xatt Ix-Xlendi • Map D2 • 2156 2951 • € • www.vjborg.com/stpatricks*

4 San Andrea, Ix-Xlendi, Gozo

Modern, but traditional in style, with archways and iron grilles. It's cosy and intimate, with 28 pretty rooms. There are great views from the roof deck but no pool. The location can't be beaten. ⚲ *St Xlendi Promenade • Map D2 • 2156 5555 • € • www.hotelsanandrea.com*

5 Maria Giovanna Guesthouse, Gozo

A delightful budget option, this traditional stone townhouse has been refurbished and each room now has en-suite facilities. Marsalforn's restaurants and nightlife are nearby and it's also easy to get away into the country. ⚲ *Marsalforn Bay • Map E1 • 2155 3630 • €€ • www.tamariagozo.com*

6 Cavalieri Hotel, St Julian's

This four-star hotel with spacious rooms is situated at the tip of St Julian's Bay, next to Spinola Bay. Its waterfront location offers great views and close proximity to many restaurants, bars and shops. There's an outdoor pool and another pool plus Jacuzzi inside. ⚲ *Spinola Road • Map N1 • 2318 0000 • €€ • www.cavalierihotel.com.mt*

7 Waterfront Hotel, Tas-Sliema

A shiny, modern seafront hotel with views across to Valletta. There's a small rooftop pool with deck, and two good restaurants overlooking the bay. You can order picnic lunches. ⚲ *Triq x-Xatt, Il-Gżira • Map M3 • 2133 3434 • €€ • www.waterfronthotel.com.mt*

8 Victoria Hotel, Tas-Sliema

The Victoria has an elegant interior evoking a 19th-century gentlemen's club. It has a courtyard pool and small sun terrace. The hotel has been certified eco-friendly by the Malta tourism authority. ⚲ *Triq Ġorġ Borġ Olivier • Map Q2 • 2133 4711 • €€€ • www.victoriahotel.com*

9 Corinthia Marina Hotel, St Julian's

A bright and airy hotel conveniently situated in St George's Bay. All rooms have private balconies with panoramic views of the bay. The hotel's pools and beach are shared with the Corinthia Hotel next door. ⚲ *St George's Bay • Map D3 • 2138 1719 • €€€€ • www.corinthiahotels.com*

10 Gillieru Harbour, St Paul's Bay

A modest, simple, and friendly hotel close to the harbour. Some rooms have splendid views. There's an excellent restaurant, a small pool, and a breezy sun terrace. Good value. ⚲ *Church Square • Map C3 • 2157 2720 • €€ • www.gillieru.com*

Price Categories

For a standard,	€ under €60
double room per	€€ €60–€120
night (with breakfast	€€€ €120–€180
if included), taxes	€€€€ €180–€240
and extra charges.	€€€€€ over €240

Cornucopia Hotel

🔟 Family-friendly Hotels

1 Westin Dragonara Resort, St Julian's

One of Malta's most lavish resorts, the vast Dragonara has something for all, including health and beauty facilities, a private beach, and all-year family entertainment – from sports tournaments to painting lessons. There are colouring books in the restaurants and electrical outlet covers in bedrooms.
🏨 Triq Dragonara • Map D3 • 2138 1000 • €€€ • www.westinmalta.com

2 Bay Street Hotel, St Julian's

Ideal for families with teenagers, this is part of a large shopping and entertainment complex, near the buzzy nightlife of Paceville. Family rooms and studio apartments with small kitchenettes are available. There's a rooftop pool and a small spa and beauty centre.
🏨 Bay Street Complex, St George's Bay • Map D3 • 2138 4421 • €€ • www.baystreet.com.mt/hotel

3 Dolmen Resort Hotel, St Paul's Bay

This smart establishment is named after the megalithic remains in the gardens. There are good-value family rooms and a summer Kids' Club with all kinds of activities. Parents can relax at the spa and there are four pools set in lush gardens.
🏨 Qawra • Map C3 • 2355 2355 • €€ • www.dolmen.com.mt

4 Ramla Bay Resort, Marfa

Situated on a small bay, this hotel is good for families who want a quiet break. There are indoor and outdoor pools, a safe sandy beach, and good water-sports facilities, but the nearest towns are a bus-ride away.
🏨 Triq Il-Marfa • Map B2 • 2281 2281 • €€ • www.ramlabayresort.com

5 Hotel Riu Seabank & Spa, Il-Mellieħa

Just across the road from this modern hotel is probably the best sandy beach in Malta, with water-sports, lidos, bars and cafés. The hotel has a jungle-themed restaurant, outdoor pool, gym and sauna, and bowling alley.
🏨 Triq Il-Marfa • Map B2 • 2289 1000 • €€€ • www.seabankhotel.com

6 Solana Hotel, Il-Mellieħa

The modern, traditional-style Solana has indoor and outdoor pools, a games room, and weekly summer barbecues. Its diving school offers special children's courses.
🏨 Triq Gorg Borg Olivier • Map B2 • 2152 2209 • €€ • www.solanahotel.com

7 Paradise Bay Resort Hotel, Ċirkewwa

This large, pink-painted hotel near the Malta-Gozo ferry terminal has its own beach. Its modest rooms are good value, and there are child-friendly restaurants, four pools, a games room, and summer barbecues.
🏨 Paradise Bay • Map A2 • 2152 1166 • €€ • www.paradise-bay.com

8 Cornucopia, Ix-Xagħra, Gozo

A converted farmhouse forms the heart of this complex, set around a flower-filled courtyard with a pool; there's also a children's pool. It has family rooms and suites.
🏨 Triq Gnien Imrik • Map E1 • 2155 6486 • €€ • www.vjborg.com/cornucopia

9 Xlendi Hotel and Resort

The Xlendi Hotel overlooks the spectacular Xlendi Bay. Spa facilities include a sauna, indoor pool and hot tub. It also has a pool on the roof, and a restaurant on the roof terrace. All rooms have airconditioning and free Wi-Fi. 🏨 Triq San Xmun, Ix-Xlendi • Map D2 • 2155 3719 • €

10 Ambassador Hotel, St Paul's Bay

Just across the road from the sea, the Ambassador offers bright, good value accommodation, a wine bar and restaurant and a large swimming pool. There's no sandy beach, but it's only a short hop on the bus to nearby Ghadira Bay. 🏨 Xemxija • Map B3 • 2157 3870 • € • www.ambassadormalta.com

Left **Mariblu Guesthouse** Middle **Point de Vue** Right **British Hotel restaurant balcony**

🔟 Budget Hotels and Guesthouses

1 Corner Hostel, Tas-Sliema

Very close to the beach, this is an unusual accommodation option for Malta: a hostel offering both en-suite rooms and dormitories, and a communal kitchen. 🕲 *6 St Margaret Street, Tas-Sliema • Map P2 • 2780 2780 • € • www. cornerhostelmalta.com*

2 The Gardens, Ir-Rabat/Victoria, Gozo

Gozo's capital has little accommodation of any kind, but this guesthouse on the outskirts is well sited for exploring the island. It's an informal set-up, with five rooms sharing two bathrooms, the kitchen, and a roof garden. 🕲 *Kercem Road • Map D2 • 2155 3723 • € • www.casalgoholidays.com*

3 Soleado Guesthouse, Tas-Sliema

This friendly, family-run guesthouse is in the heart of Tas-Sliema's nightlife and shopping area, so it's a good choice for young travellers on a budget. It offers rooms with or without en-suite facilities. 🕲 *Triq Ghar Id-Dud • Map Q2 • 2133 4415 • € • www. soleadomalta.com*

4 British Hotel, Valletta

The gloomy, 1970s-style lobby belies the bright rooms upstairs. Most have en-suite bathrooms, and the best, fine views of the Grand Harbour. (A sixth-floor room with a sea view costs extra.) Give the hotel restaurant a miss, but head for the roof bar at sunset. 🕲 *40 Triq Il-Batterija • Map J3 • 2122 4730 • €€ • www.britishhotel.com*

5 Hostel Jones, Tas-Sliema

Set in an ideal location, Hostel Jones is headed by a young team that lends it a fresh vibe. It offers great value for money and excellent facilities, with rooms that have a distinct appeal. 🕲 *Sir Adrian Dingli Street • Map P2 • 9932 0003 • €*

6 Point de Vue, Ir-Rabat (Malta)

Book ahead for rooms in this family-run guesthouse just outside the main gate to the "Silent City". 🕲 *2/7 Is-Saqqajja • Map C4 • 2145 4117 • €€ • www.pointdevuemalta.com*

7 Lantern Guesthouse, Marsalforn, Gozo

This is one of the most appealing budget options in Marsalforn, offering simple en-suite rooms and basic apartments – good value for families or groups. There is a small fee for airconditioning, but the rooms have fans. Inexpensive restaurant and pizzeria downstairs. 🕲 *Triq Qbajjar • Map E1 • 2155 6285 • € • www.gozo.com/lantern*

8 Mariblu Guesthouse, Ix-Xewkija, Gozo

This is a friendly, family-run guesthouse in a sleepy Gozitan village famous for its parish church *(see p39)*. The rooms, all with en-suite bathrooms, are above the Mariblu restaurant in the village centre. There are two swimming pools, and a dive centre. 🕲 *Mgarr Road • Map E2 • 2155 1315 • € • www.mariblugozo.com*

9 Primera Hotel, Buġibba

Modern and functional, the Primera Hotel has a good central location and reasonable facilities for the price. There are indoor and outdoor pools, a kids' paddling pool, and a rooftop terrace for sunbathing. Rooms are plain, but equipped with air-conditioning and satellite TV. 🕲 *Pioneer Rd • Map C3 • 2157 3880 • €€ • www.primerahotel.com*

10 Splendid Guesthouse, Il-Mellieħa

Pristine rooms (each with a shower or full en-suite facilities), a buzzy little bar and restaurant, free Wi-Fi, a small sun terrace and charming owners make this the best budget deal in Il-Mellieħa. The beach is a short bus-ride away, but shops and nightlife are close by. 🕲 *Triq Kappillan Magri • Map B3 • 2152 1326 • €€ • www.splendidmalta.com*

Many of Gozo's traditional farmhouses have been restored and are rented to visitors as self-catering accommodation.

Price Categories

For a standard, double room per night (with breakfast if included), taxes and extra charges.

€ under €60
€€ €60–€120
€€€ €120–€180
€€€€ €180–€240
€€€€€ over €240

Comino Hotel Bungalows

📟 Self-catering Accommodation

1 Comino Hotel Bungalows

Neat rows of pink-and peach-painted bungalows overlook Comino's prettiest beach. They are linked via a panoramic, cliffside path to the Comino Hotel *(see p114)*, whose sports facilities and private beach they share. ❧ *Santa Marija Bay • Map F2 • 2152 9821 • Open Apr–Oct • €*
• www.cominohotel.com

2 Gozo Prestige Holidays, L-Għarb

This reliable local business offers 16 magnificent Gozitan farmhouses for rent, all in idyllic locations near pretty villages. They are furnished in rustic style and boast pools with Jacuzzis, barbecue areas, fully equipped kitchens, and multilingual TV. ❧ *Triq San Pietru • Map D1 • 9946 7860 • €€€ • www.gozo. com/prestige holidays*

3 Palazzo Prince d'Orange, Valletta

A beautiful palazzo constructed in the 17th century, this building has retained many of its original Baroque features. It now has several apartments providing all luxury facilities. ❧ *St Paul's Street • Map J3 • 9984 6615 • €€€ • www.palazzo princemalta.com*

4 Mellieħa Holiday Centre

This large Danish-run tourist village sits just behind Mellieħa Bay. Its tastefully designed limestone bungalows and studios are set in gardens. The facilities include bars and restaurants, two pools (one for children), a tennis court, mini-golf, and a games room.
❧ *Ghadira Bay • Map B3 • 2289 3000 • € • www. melliehaholidaycentre.com*

5 Gozo Farmhouses, Għajnsielem

Beautiful farmhouses across Gozo have been restored using traditional techniques, and furnished luxuriously. Some boast antique four-poster beds and Jacuzzis; all have private pools. Food packs can be provided, or even a private chef to prepare local dishes. ❧ *3 Mgarr Road • Map E2 • 2156 1280 • €€ • www.gozofarm houses.com*

6 Holiday Malta

This locally based online agency can organize self-catering apartments, farmhouses, and villas. It's particularly good for areas with few hotels or guesthouses, and also has characterful Valetta accommodation. ❧ *€€ • www.holiday-malta.com*

7 Valletta Studios

Quaint and unusual studio apartments with views of the Grand Harbour. One boasts an original wood-panelled box gallery, typical of Valletta's architecture. Extras such as CD- and DVD-players make them feel like a home from home. ❧ *63 Triq Il-Batterija • Map J3 • 2702 1656 • €€ • www.vallettastudios.com*

8 Dar Ta' Zeppi, Il-Qala, Gozo

This charming, artistically restored house has two spacious rooms, each big enough for a family and with kitchenettes. Prices include at least breakfast, but you can cook other meals yourself. ❧ *39 28th April 1688 St • Map F2 • 2155 5051 • €€ • www. dartazeppi.com*

9 Villa Renters

This large, UK-based web company has a wide range of farmhouses and villas for rent. You then contact the owners direct and pay by credit card. ❧ *www.villa-holiday.co.uk*

10 Pebbles Boutique Aparthotel, Tas-Sliema

Pebbles offers apartments on the seafront with free Wi-Fi and a rooftop terrace. In summer, it also runs the Pebbles Lido, 1 km (half a mile) away, which has two sea water pools, a children's pool, and a water-sports centre with everything from banana boat rides to yacht charter. ❧ *88-89 Triq Ix-Xatt • Map Q3 • 2131 1889 • € • www.mol.net.mt/pebbles*

General Index

General Index

General Index

Acknowledgements

The Author
Mary-Ann Gallagher is a widely experienced travel writer, now based in Barcelona. She has written and contributed to several Dorling Kindersley titles including *Top 10 Costa Blanca* and *RealCity Barcelona*, as well as guides for other publishers to Crete, Vienna and many other destinations.

The author wishes to thank all in Malta who provided her with invaluable help, among them: Shirley Psaila at the Maltese tourist office; Pierre Cassar at Heritage Malta; Mario Farrugia at Fondazzjoni Wirt Artna; Jo Balzan at St John's Co-Cathedral; Stephen Cini at Gozo's Museum of Archae-ology; Tanya van Poucke and her delightful family at Dar ta Zeppi; Freddie at the Animal Sanctuary; and Lucia Mizzi.

Produced by Coppermill Books, 55 Salop Road London E17 7HS
Editorial Director Chris Barstow
Designer Ian Midson
Copy Editor Michael Wright
Proofreader Antony Mason
Fact-checker Christine Debono
Indexer Hilary Bird

Main Photographer Antony Souter
Additional Photography Rough Guides/Victor Borg 73tl, Ruth Chircop, Rough Guides/Eddie Gerald, Rough Guides/Antony Souter 72tl
Illustrator Chapel Design & Marketing
Maps Dominic Beddow and Simonetta Giori at Draughtsman Maps
Cartography Credits Mapping for Malta and Gozo derived from the Mapping Unit, Malta Environment and Planning Authority (MEPA)

FOR DORLING KINDERSLEY
Publisher Douglas Amrine
Publishing Manager Vivien Antwi
Design Manager Karen Constanti
Senior Cartographic Editor Casper Morris
DTP Designer Natasha Lu
Production Controller Linda Dare
Revisions Team Louise Abbott, Ashwin Raju Adimari, Claire Baranowski, Antoine Borg, Jo Caruana, Ruth Chircop, Rhiannon Furbear, Claire Jones, Cincy Jose, Rahul Kumar, Maite Lantaron, Jude Ledger, Nicola Malone, Lucia Mizzi, Catherine Palmi, Ellen Root, Susanne Hillen, Ajay Verma, Hugo Wilkinson

Picture Credits
Placement Key: a-above; b-below/bottom; c-centre; f-far; l-left; r-right; t-top.

The publishers would like to thank the following individuals, companies and picture libraries for their kind permission to reproduce their photographs.

ALAMY IMAGES: Greg Balfour Evans 53bl, 72tr. ARRIVA: 106TR; BRIDGE-MAN ART LIBRARY: Private Collection 13clb, Bibliothèque Nationale, Paris 13br. CAFÉ JUBILEE: 66tr. corinthia hotel st. georges bay: 74tr. DANIEL CILIA: 7tr, 22cla, 22c, 22br, 23tr, 23ca, 23bc, 93c. DREAMSTIME.COM: Spectral-design 49cl. GETTY IMAGES-HULTON ARCHIVE: 33cl, Stringer/Sacha Steinbech 40tr. MALTA TOURISM AUTHORITY: 48tl, 48tr, 48bl, 49tr, 49br. POINT DE VUE: 116tc. raffael restaurant: 75tl.

All other images are © Dorling Kindersley. For further information see *www.dkimages.com*

Phrase Book

Virtually everyone in Malta is bilingual and speaks Malti and English with equal fluency. Locals don't expect visitors to be able to speak Malti, but appreciate efforts to say a few words in their language. The written Maltese language uses some unsual characters – some letters are crossed and others have a dot. This means that some place names, for example, can be hard to pronounce without a little help.

Maltese Pronunciation Key

ċ - as ch in church
e – as in get
g – (hard) as in good
ġ - (soft) as in gentle
h – usually silent
ħ – as "h" in hand
i – (long) as "ee", e.g. see
j – as "y" in yacht
gh – usually silent
q – silent
x – (soft) as "sh", e.g. sheep
ż - (soft) as in zebra
z – as "ts", e.g. cats

In an Emergency

Get the police	**Sejjah pulizija**	sey-yah pul-its-iya
Danger	**Periklu**	peh-ree-klu
Fire	**Nar**	nahr
Get a doctor	**Sejjah tabib**	sey-yah tab-eeb
Go away	**Mur 'l hemm**	moor lemm
Help	**Ajjut**	eye-ut
I'm lost	**Intlift**	int-lift
Police	**Pulizija**	poo-lee-tsee-yah

Communication Essentials

Yes	**Iva**	ee-vah
No	**Le**	leh
Please	**Jekk joghgbok**	yek yoj-bok
Thank you	**Grazzi**	grah-tsi
very much	**hafna**	ha-fnah
You're	**M'hemmx**	memsh
welcome	**mn'hiex**	mneesh
Good morning	**Bongu**	bohn-joo
Good evening	**Bonswa**	bohn-swar
Good night	**Il-lejl it-tajjeb**	ill-ale ee-tay-eb
Good-bye	**Sahha**	sah-ha
So long	**Caw**	chow
See you later	**Narak iktar tard**	nah-rak ik-tah tard
Sorry!	**Skuzani!**	skoo-zah-nee
Where?	**Fejn?**	fayn

How?	**Kif?**	keef
When?	**Meta?**	meh-tah
What?	**X'hini?**	sheen-eey
Why?	**Ghaliex?**	ah-leesh
Who?	**Min?**	meen
Which?	**Liema?**	lee-mah

Useful Phrases

Pleased to	**Ghandi**	ahn-dee pee-
meet you	**pjacir**	yach-eer
How are you?	**Kif inti?**	keef een-tee
Very well, thanks	**Tajjeb, grazzi**	tay-eb, grah-zee
And you?	**hafna U**	haf-nah oo
	inti?	een-tee
I beg your	**Skuzi?**	skoo-zee
pardon?		
Excuse me	**Skuzi!**	skoo-zee
Where is...?	**Fejn hu...?**	fayn oo
Where are...?	**Fejn huma?**	fayn oo-mah
Where can I	**Fejn nista**	feyn nee-stah
find?	**insib?**	een-seeb
How long...?	**Kemm iddum?**	kehm ee-duhm
How much/	**Kemm...?**	kehm
many?		
How much is	**Kemm iqum**	kehm ee-um
this?	**dan/din?**	dahn/deen
Do you speak	**Titkellem**	teet-keh-luhm
English?	**bl-Ingliz?**	bul een-gleese
I understand	**Nifhem**	nee-fehm
I don't	**Ma nifhimx**	mah nee-fimsh
understand		
Can you	**Tista' tghinni?**	tis-tah tay-nee
help?		
I'd like	**Nixtieq**	nish-ti
We'd like	**Nixtiequ**	nish-ti-oo
I'm lost	**Intlift**	eent-leeft
Happy	**Il-Milied**	eel mee-leed
Christmas!	**it-Tajjeb!**	eet-tay-eb
Happy New	**Is-Sena**	iss-ehn-nah
Year!	**t-Tajba!**	eet-tay-bah
Happy Easter!	**L-Ghid it-Tajjeb!**	layd eet tay-eb
Best Wishes!	**Xewqat Sbieh!**	shew-aht sbee
Congratulations!	**Nifrahlek!**	nee-frah-rah-lek
Good luck!	**Ix-Xorti**	ish-shore-tee
	t-Tajba!	eet-tay-bah

Numbers

0	**xejn**	shayn
1	**wiehed**	wee-het
2	**tnejn**	tneyn
3	**tlieta**	tleetah

4	**erbgħa**	ehr-bah
5	**ħamsa**	hum-sah
6	**sitta**	sit-tah
7	**sebgħa**	seh-bah
8	**tmienja**	tmeen-yah
9	**disgħa**	diss-ah
10	**għaxra**	ahsh-rah
11	**ħdax**	hdahsh
12	**tnax**	tnahsh
13	**tlettax**	tlet-tahsh
14	**erbatax**	ehr-bah-tahsh
15	**ħmistax**	hmiss-tahsh
16	**sittax**	sit-tash
17	**sbatax**	zbah-tahsh
18	**tmintax**	tmin-tahsh
19	**dsatax**	tsa-tahsh
20	**għoxrin**	aw-shreen
21	**wieħed u**	wee-het oo
	għoxrin	aw-shreen
22	**tnejn u**	tneyn oo
	għoxrin	aw-shreen
30	**tletin**	tle-teen
40	**erbgħin**	er-beyn
50	**ħamsin**	hum-seen
60	**sittin**	sit-teen
70	**sebgħin**	se-beyn
80	**tmenin**	tmen-een
90	**disgħin**	dee-seyn
100	**mija**	mee-yah
1,000	**elf**	elf
1,000,000	**miljun**	mill-yoon

Pronunciation of Place Names

Some places – for example, those with Italian names like Valletta – are pronounced just as they are spelt. But Maltese names can be tongue-twisters for visitors. Here are some of the trickier ones:

Birżebbuġa	beer-zeb-boo-jah
Buġibba	boo-jib-bah
Ċirkewwa	cheer-keh-wah
Dwejra	dway-rah
Ġgantija	ja-gun-tee-yah
Ħaġar Qim	ha-jar-qeem
Ħal Luqa	hull-loo-qah
Ħal Tarxien	hull-tahr-shin
Il-Mellieħa	ill-mell-ee-hah
Il-Qawra	ill-qow-rah
In-Naxxar	In-nahsh-shar
Is-Siġġiewi	iss-sidge-ee-wee
Ix-Xagħra	ish-shah-rah
Ix-Xewkija	ish-show-kee-jah
Ix-Xlendi	ish-shlen-dee
L-Għarb	lahrb
L-Imdina	lim-dee-nah
L-Imġarr	lim-jar
L-Imsida	lim-see-dah
Marsaxlokk	marsah-shlock
Paceville	pah-che-vill

Valletta Street Names

Most street signs are in Malti, but it's worth being familiar with their English equivalents; most shops and businesses use them, some maps are in English only – and you may simply find it easier to say South St than Triq Nofs In-Nhar. Here is a selective list:

Britannja, Triq	Brittania St
Girolamo Cassar, Triq	Girolamo Cassar St
Id-Dejqa, Triq	Strait St
Il-Batterija, Triq	Battery St
Il-Fontana, Triq	Fountain St
Il-Fran, Triq	Old Bakery St
Il-Mall	The Mall
Il-Mediterran, Triq	Mediterranean St
Il-Merkanti, Triq	Merchant's St
Il-Punent, Triq	West St
Ir-Repubblika, Misraħ	Republic Sq
Ir-Repubblika, Triq	Republic St
It-Teatru L'Antik, Triq	Old Theatre St
Kastilja, Misraħ	Castille Sq
L-4 Ta' Settembru, Misraħ	4th September Sq
L-Arċisqof, Triq	Archbishop St
L-Assedju L-Kbir, Triq	Great Siege Rd
L'Ispar Il-Quadim, Triq	Old Hospital St
Lascaris, Triq	Lascaris St
L'Imitħen, Triq	Windmill St
Marsamxett, Triq	Marsamxett St
Mattia Preti, Pjazza	Mattia Preti Sq
Melita, Triq	Melita St
Nelson, Triq	Nelson St
Nofs In-Nhar, Triq	South St
Papa Benedittu XV, Misraħ	Pope Benedict XV St
Papa Piju V, Triq	Pope Pius V
San Bastian, Triq	St Sebastian St
San Duminku, Triq	St Dominic St
San Ġwann, Misraħ	St John Sq
San Ġwann, Triq	St John St
San Kristofru, Triq	St Christoper St
San Marku, Triq	St Mark St
San Nikola, Triq	St Nicholas St
San Patrizju, Triq	St Patrick St
San Pawl, Triq	St Paul St
Sant' Anna, Triq	St Anna St
Sant' Ursula, Triq	St Ursula St
Santa Lucija, Triq	St Lucija St
Sarria, Triq	Sarria St
Zakkarija, Triq	Zachary St
Zekka, Triq	Old Mint St

Selected Map Indexes

Selected Map Indexes